WHEN YOUR KID GOES TO COLLEGE

WHEN YOUR KID GOES TO COLLEGE

A PARENTS' SURVIVAL GUIDE

CAROL BARKIN

AVON BOOKS NEW YORK

DOONESBURY cartoon © 1998 G. B. Trudeau. Reprinted with permission of UNIVERSAL PRESS SYNDICATE. All rights reserved.

AVON BOOKS, INC.
1350 Avenue of the Americas
New York, New York 10019

Copyright © 1999 by Carol Barkin
Front cover illustration by Clifford Faust
Interior design by Kellan Peck
Published by arrangement with the author
ISBN: 0-380-79840-9
www.avonbooks.com

Library of Congress Cataloging in Publication Data:

Barkin, Carol.
    When your kid goes to college : a parents' survival guide / Carol Barkin.
        p.   cm.
    Includes index.
    ISBN 0-380-79840-9 (pbk.)
    1. College student orientation—United States. 2. College students—United States—Family relationships. I. Title.
LB2343.32.B35   1999   99-11099
378.1'98—dc21   CIP

First Avon Books Trade Paperback Printing: April 1999

AVON TRADEMARK REG. U.S. PAT. OFF. AND IN OTHER COUNTRIES, MARCA REGISTRADA, HECHO EN U.S.A.

Printed in the U.S.A.

10

For Spike, whose loving support and collaboration
made an idea become reality,
and for David, my inspiration and reality check

BY GARRY TRUDEAU

ACKNOWLEDGMENTS

Authors often say their books could not have been written without other people's help and encouragement. That statement has never been truer than in my case. My husband, Spike, believed in the idea from the very beginning and offered constant enthusiasm and support. I am everlastingly grateful for his help in conducting many of the interviews and in critiquing first, second, and third drafts. Our son, David, provided much-appreciated encouragement and a welcome review from another generation's point of view. I was delighted and very proud that he agreed to write a chapter from the student's perspective.

Perhaps most important, this book could not have been begun, let alone completed, without the extraordinary generosity of many parents and kids. Their willingness to talk openly and freely about their feelings, their expectations, and their moments of disappointment and of joyful pride helped generate and refine the continuing themes of the book. I won't name names, but you all know who you are. Thank you a million times.

CONTENTS

INTRODUCTION

In the spring of my son's senior year of high school, I began meeting informally with a few other parents of seniors. We had lunch or coffee, occasionally we gathered for dinner, and we talked—about our kids and about what was in store for them and for us the following year when they went off to college. For nearly all of us this was our first or only child, and we were excited, apprehensive, and confused. We felt clueless—we didn't know what to do or how to begin to get our kids, and ourselves, ready for the separation in September.

As the summer progressed we continued to meet, now exchanging ideas for shopping and packing as well as venting frustration over our kids' sometimes surly, withdrawn, or hysterical behavior as departure time drew nearer. Our gatherings went on through the fall and, in fact, through the whole freshman year, as we listened with interest to what one another's kids were doing and how they were faring at college.

The support and sympathy during the rough times, as well as the genuine pleasure at hearing of the kids' successes, were more valuable than any of us, I think, had expected. We jokingly called ourselves a "support group," and indeed that's what we were. Comparing notes, seeing both the differences and the many similarities among our kids' experiences, offering friendly advice, and reassuring one another that our feelings were normal, helped us weather the emotional storms and cope with the small stuff.

Out of that support group came the idea for this book— to provide the same kind of support for other parents who are embarking on this exhilarating and stressful journey. The parents interviewed for the book come from a wide range of religious and ethnic backgrounds, and their kids included males and females, jocks and aesthetes, straight-A types and those who had studied just enough to get by. Some planned to live at home and commute to college, though most were going away to state universities or private colleges. And while some kids couldn't wait to spread their wings and fly, others secretly wondered about their ability to handle independence.

The experience is unique for every family, yet it's also much the same for all of us as we look for ways to simultaneously let go of our kids and stay connected to them. I hope this book will reassure you that you're not alone in your concerns; I hope, too, that it will suggest some useful ways of looking at and coping with the questions and choices all parents face when their kids go to college.

CHAPTER ONE

Summer of Anticipation

It's really happened: Your kid is about to graduate from high school, and you're looking forward to the next big step with a mixture of anxiety and excitement. Even though at times you wondered whether your family would survive the high school years—the phone calls at all hours, the clothes and shoes scattered through the house, the defiant staying out all night, and the frequent withering judgment that "you don't understand"—you're likely to feel a bit choked up as the diplomas are handed out. It seems like only yesterday that this kid started kindergarten, and trite though it sounds, you wonder where the years have flown.

Emotional Changes for Everyone

Like many parents, you may have found that your relationship with your college-bound child began to change as early as the second half of his senior year in high school.

My son got his first college acceptance in February, and all of a sudden he was transformed. It was partly relief—he felt, At least someone wants me; I won't be rejected everywhere. He became much more pleasant to be around, more responsible about a lot of things. He actually sat down and talked with us once in a while.

Lots of kids seem suddenly more grown-up at this point, and there are good reasons for it. They can drive, they're at the top of the high school ladder, they probably know where they're going next year, and they're becoming aware that their lives from now on will be quite different from before. The end of high school represents the end of an era for a child, the end of a particular way of living with others in a family—in many ways, the end of childhood.

Parents, of course, know that it's not really the end of childhood; there's still a long road ahead of gradually diminishing dependence, both emotional and financial. And they know, too, that change is necessary: Children have to grow up, and in their calmer moments parents don't actually want to treat an eighteen-year-old the way they treated a toddler. But knowing it has to happen doesn't always make it easy to accept.

So, as the names are called out at high school commencement, you may be anxious as well as proud. If this is the first child you're sending to college, you may feel you have no idea what to expect or how to prepare. Even if you've already been through it, the experience is different each time.

The first time is the hardest, but in some ways I was more ready for my older daughter to leave. She was more difficult with me all along. She started to separate in January; by September I knew it was time for her to move on. I was actually more upset about my younger daughter leaving. I guess I saw her as less prepared, just because she was younger. She only began to separate from us a couple of weeks before she went to college, and I wondered if she was ready for the whole thing.

The summer before your kid's first year of college can be pretty hard for everyone. The reality sinks in: In just a few weeks you'll be sending your child into a new environment, a new stage of her life. Even if she'll be living at home and commuting to college, her life, and yours, will be different from the way it was while she was in high school. And if she's going away to school, she'll be out of your house and on her own in a way she hasn't been before.

Looking this prospect in the face makes you realize you're getting older—old enough to have a child in college, which marks a new stage in your life as well as your child's. For some parents this is a liberating realization; they look forward to having more time and freedom to pursue their own interests or move in a new career direction. For others it can be a bit frightening; if their lives have revolved around their role as parents, they foresee the loss of their emotional focus and perhaps of a network of established social relationships connected with their child's school and friends. Either way, the impending changes can create tension as you begin to look at your family from a different perspective.

I planned to go back to school as soon as my son left for college, to fulfill an old ambition of becoming a landscape designer. I thought it would be good for me to have something to throw myself into so I wouldn't feel at loose ends. But I was nervous about it all summer and so distracted that I probably didn't give him the attention he needed. Actually, I don't remember much about what the summer was like.

Whatever their plans, or lack thereof, for the fall, lots of parents find that this precollege summer slips by much too fast. Before they know it, it's July: Labor Day and college orientation week seem just around the corner. Many feel an urgent need to make this last summer of childhood perfect—quality time in every way.

My daughter was home all summer, and it was really important to me that everything be special and memorable for her. I envisioned lots of family dinners and barbecues with every-

body full of warmth and good feelings, and I planned to have all these quiet heart-to-heart talks with her, maybe on long walks in the park. I just kept wanting to fill her up with good advice so she'd be able to make the transition smoothly. And I guess I was hoping to reinforce the family bonds before she left so she wouldn't forget us.

It sounds great, but don't count on it. Things don't often work out quite this ideally. Most kids are extremely nervous before they set off to college, and their nervousness comes out in different ways, not all of which are attractive. Many seem to slide back to an earlier stage; it's as if their fears about the future make them want to pull the cocoon of childhood up over their heads again. They refuse to talk or even think about college, and they resist everything that might force them to acknowledge it as an impending reality—such as packing, choosing courses, even sending in required forms about mundane topics like meal plans. They're irritable or sullen, snapping when spoken to or entirely uncommunicative.

This behavior is hard to live with, and parents feel frustrated and worried: Will this child, who can't even deal with the preliminary steps, be able to cope with college life?

The hardest time we had was the summer before he left; there were definitely rough spots. He did rebellious things he hadn't done before, almost as though he was angry. I didn't understand it at first, but then I thought, it's a good time for this to happen, we're ready to separate!

Your child's behavior may be bewildering and painful to you. But a kid who looks for reasons to pick fights with his parents all summer long may actually be looking for a way to cover up his fears and his sadness about leaving. If he's mad at you, it will feel, on the surface at least, a whole lot easier to go away.

On the other hand, some kids seem to suddenly **mature**

during the summer. Sounding rational and eager, they hold long discussions with their parents about the challenges in store; it's as if they wake up one day and say, "I'm ready." Naturally parents see this as reassuring evidence that their children will manage the transition to college successfully. In fact, of course, very few of them truly feel unmixed confidence about their ability to cope with an unknown future. But teenagers are pretty good at putting on a "game face," and doing so helps them reassure themselves as well as their parents.

Still, however superficial the mask, it's hard to face the prospect of such kids leaving home just as they're turning into responsible citizens. One mother said:

> *During the summer my daughter became very nice, very sweet and appreciative—a pleasure to have around. I think she saw it was the end of an era.*

The most common summer behavior seems to combine both extremes. One day your child acts totally put together, looking over the college catalog and making realistic-sounding plans; the next day she can't remember where she put the questionnaire about roommate preferences that has to be returned by tomorrow, and she responds to your questions about it with an angry "Leave me alone!"

It's hard to deal with this. On the one hand, you don't want to spend all summer nagging and quarreling; that certainly doesn't fit your hoped-for scenario of serious and satisfying discussions about life. On the other hand, you feel you have a right to be interested and concerned; you're still her parent, you're probably paying for her education, and you can't stand to see her getting off to a scatterbrained start. Also, like every other parent, you want a chance to arm your child with advice based on your own knowledge and experience, and to reaffirm your connection before your son or daughter flies off into a new world without you.

I wanted to spend a lot of time with my kid before she left. I thought it was important to make opportunities to be together and to share feelings before this momentous step. But she was uncomfortable with anything like that, and finally I realized I was probably making things worse for her, even if not for me.

It helps to remind yourself that your child is going through a tremendous emotional upheaval, full of contradictory pushes and pulls. Underneath the excitement of being a high school graduate—a major step into adulthood—kids can't help being scared. They worry about everything from whether they'll be able to handle the academic work at college to what kinds of clothes they'll need. Many college students remember that two major questions preoccupied them all summer long: Did I choose the right school, and will I fit in and make friends? Such concerns are inevitable, and when you think about it, you'd be worried, too, about your ability to handle a new and unknown way of life.

Though they may not want to acknowledge it, most kids are also feeling sad that their childhood is drawing to an end, and terrified at the realization that they'll soon be giving up the security of life as a child at home. Even kids who might be expected to be eager to leave—those who had a difficult time in high school, socially or academically, or who had troubles at home—are scared. They may feel they can't wait to move on and start over, but they also wonder if they'll make a success of this new stage of life.

The whole process of college application and admission sometimes seems designed to intensify, rather than allay, such anxieties. It's nearly impossible not to perceive the application process as a competition; kids can't help hoping to do better than, or at least as well as, their friends, especially if they've applied to the same colleges, and they suffer agonies of wondering whether they're smart enough and competent enough to succeed. Parents, too, have spent months worrying that their child will be rejected and that his unique qualities won't be recognized. And if he didn't get into his first-choice college, both child and parent may feel defensive when friends ask where he's going. At times like this it's important to remember the truths every college guidance counselor repeats: There's no single "right" school, and what's best for one student isn't necessarily best for another.

The unstable mix of excitement and apprehension escalates as the summer goes on, and it can produce sudden blowups for no apparent reason. It's typical for kids to have so much to do to get ready to leave that they end up doing none of it, or at least none that parents can see. Meanwhile, it's hard for parents to give up control, and this often results in a lot of nagging.

But looked at from another angle, a kid's procrastination may be partly designed to elicit nagging from parents. Why would anyone do this? One reason might be to make it easier to leave home: The child can feel, At last I'm getting out of here, I can't wait to get away from my parents' need to run my life. For another kid, though, the nagging may represent welcome proof that she's still a child enveloped in her parents' protective arms; this can be reassuring for someone who's not sure she can cope with being a grown-up yet.

Some kids recognize their own mixed feelings and can actually admit their fears.

My son was openly anxious all summer about what going to college would be like. He was able to talk about feeling anxious, and he spent hours reading everything the college sent to him. I think the talking and the reading helped somewhat, but he was still very nervous.

Many try to conceal their feelings, though, from themselves as well as from their families. They're trying hard to be independent and self-sufficient; acknowledging that they are afraid would feel like a retreat to a time when Mom and Dad could make everything better. So the kid who appears calm and in control may be striving to conceal his fears and self-doubts under an "adult" facade, while the kid who

behaves like a willful four-year-old may be acting out the
dependent-child role one last time. He may also be testing
his parents' patience and acceptance: Will you still love me
if I'm not as grown-up as everyone thinks I should be? And
even the kid who recognizes that he's being difficult may
seem unable to stop himself.

> *My son and I didn't get along the whole summer. He was
> testing in ways he never did before—not showing up where
> he was supposed to be, not calling, not doing things he'd
> promised to do. He needed to establish some distance, and
> that's how he dealt with it. In between he'd say, "I don't mean
> to be like this, I'm sorry I'm giving you a hard time," and
> then he'd go on and give me a hard time again.*

Another contributing cause of a kid's difficult behavior
can be a genuine concern about how her parents will deal
with her departure. A child may worry that parents will be
lonely without her and will spend too much time worrying
about her when she's not at home. But it's hard to express
this feeling directly.

> *My daughter was obnoxious all summer, but sometimes she
> could step back and see what was happening. She even said
> once, "Mom, there's a reason I'm acting this way—it will
> make it easier for you to have me leave."*

The space between high school and college can feel like
an unpredictable limbo for a kid. He doesn't want to be
treated as a child, but he's scared of the adult role, so he
swings back and forth between anger at being patronized
by adults and fear that he'll be expected to act like an adult
himself. No wonder he's snappish from time to time!

For other kids, though, the emotional ups and downs
seem almost nonexistent, or at least submerged. An interesting summer job can be a tremendous help.

My son had a job downtown for the summer. He was glad to be working, he enjoyed dressing up for work, having responsi-bilities—it felt like being in the real world.

Even a boring job takes up time that might otherwise be spent worrying.

My daughter couldn't wait to get out of high school—she didn't have a great senior year—but she was pretty nervous and scared about what college would be like (she's commuting and living at home). But she worked at a fast-food place most of the summer, so she didn't have time to worry. When we got back from vacation, she was ready for the real world.

If your child decides to go away for the summer—as a counselor at a sleep-away camp, for example—you may feel hurt, deprived of the last few weeks of family life the way it's always been. But some kids need a "trial separation" before the big one. Being away from home for the summer provides a chance to see how it feels, with the security of knowing it's only for a short time.

The Summer Speeds Up

Now the last weeks of summer are flying by, much too fast, and you still don't feel you have a handle on things. Talking to other parents can be enormously useful, especially if they have kids already in college. But sometimes friends are a good deal less helpful than you hope.

One of the big problems was that everyone was asking my daughter questions: Where are you going to college, what will you major in, what have you bought to take with you, won't you need this or that? No conversation with an adult this summer was about anything else—there was no way to get away from it. Both of us would have preferred not to discuss it all the time, to just live our life and pretend this was a regular summer, but it was impossible. In the supermarket, at the pool, everyplace we met anybody, this was the discussion— have you got your boxes yet, what are you taking to school? It drove us both crazy, but especially my daughter.

These aren't malicious questions. People are just taking an interest in what's going on in your life, but it can feel overwhelming. Your child will appreciate being shielded from the onslaught as much as possible—this is one time when you can answer on your kid's behalf with impunity. And you can turn the ubiquitousness of the topic to your advantage. Ask a persistent questioner how she dealt with the particular issue she's inquiring about: How did she and her child solve the problem of desk lamps or storage space or shipping a computer to college? You may pick up some useful information while you give your kid some breathing space.

As the end of summer approaches, you may notice that you're not seeing much of your kid. All your plans for family togetherness come up against your child's seeming need to spend every possible moment with his high school friends. He's out late every night, and when he's home he's on the phone.

The summer before my son went to college, his social life was out of control. It was a combination of excitement and anxiety, I think; he had to see his friends all the time. It was very hectic.

For kids like this, the frenzied social life is probably necessary. They're suddenly realizing that this particular group of friends won't be together in the same way ever again, and they have to jam in as much time together as possible.

My daughter wanted to stay home this summer to be with her friends—they all had local jobs. They were very emotional all summer, mourning the past, being together a lot. They all talked about not being as ready to leave as they thought they'd be, about how much they'd all wanted to get away from home when they were sixteen and now they were feeling more tentative. Before they even left, there was more feeling of loss than they'd expected.

Parents often find themselves irritated at their kid's total involvement with friends during this time. They feel rejected, as if they're being pushed out of their child's life long before it's necessary. And they don't always cope with it well.

I was upset that my son was out every minute and had no time for his family, and we did a lot of yelling at each other. Of course I felt terrible every time that happened. I'd wanted him to have happy memories of the summer, and now all he was going to remember was me screaming at him.

A little screaming won't ruin your relationship with your kid, but if it gets out of hand, try to step back and remember that your child's friends have probably been a big part of his life for a long time. The prospect of leaving makes many kids realize how strong the ties are and how much they'll miss the familiarity and comfort of these friendships. They tend to assume that though their family will always be there, their relationships with their friends will come to an end as soon as they disperse to different colleges. This prediction may not come true, but at the moment it feels as if a safety net is about to be snatched away.

A boyfriend or girlfriend who's going to a different college adds another source of confusion for your kid; the two of them anticipate the pain of being apart and may cling together as much as they can before they separate. At the same time, high school couples know that the odds are against their staying together once college starts and they meet new people. Some break up during the summer, perhaps to get it over with before the uncertainties of college overwhelm them.

My daughter had a relationship with a boy in high school, and a lot of her summer was spent dealing with leaving that relationship. It became much more volatile, they fought with each other in order to be able to leave each other. Yet she was very anxious about life without him.

Sometimes the decision to break up isn't mutual. When this happens, the cloud of sullen moodiness and irritability can loom very large. Being rejected by a boyfriend or girl-friend can intensify a kid's insecurity about the new social scene that lies ahead. And, as many parents already know, it doesn't help much to trot out clichés like "there are lots of good fish in the sea," which sounds as if you're dismissing the importance of a relationship your kid took very seriously. Still less helpful are comments like "I never liked him anyway; you'll find someone better at college." Though you intend to help your kid get over her sadness with this "good riddance" message, it sounds to her as if you're questioning her judgment and taste while demonstrating that you knew best all along. Neutral sympathy—"I know it's hard and that you're feeling sad"—is about the only useful thing you can offer while you wait for the emotional storm to subside.

On the other hand, you may find that your child is outgrowing his high school group and is ready to move on.

Most of the summer my son was moody and stressed out. He said, "There's nothing to do here, I can't wait to get out of this place." He was restless, bored with his job, and counting the days until he could leave for college. I think it was because he didn't have deep roots here with his high school group—I don't think he felt he was leaving that much behind.

It's reassuring to feel that your child is looking forward to new experiences and a wider choice of companions, but the mood swings almost every kid goes through can make daily life something of a trial in an already difficult and stressful time.

> *I told a friend, "This summer has been horrible—my daughter is so unpleasant to be around! She's cranky and tired all the time, and she bites my head off whenever I make any attempt to talk to her." My friend, whose kid is a year older than mine, said, "Oh, I know, they're all like that before they go to college. My daughter was horrible, too." I felt so relieved to know that it wasn't something wrong with my kid, or with me.*

Divorced parents often feel extra pressure and anxieties. If your child doesn't live with you, you may feel you have to make every minute of togetherness count, and the pressure to do this can backfire, cranking tensions even higher. Decisions about college—how it will be paid for and by whom, and who's in charge of what—can provide rich ground for playing out old, unresolved issues between divorced parents. Naturally it's best for everyone, especially your kid, if all of you can discuss things calmly and lower the stress level as much as possible.

It often helps to keep responsibilities clearly separate. One divorced mother bought towels, sheets, and laundry basics while her ex-husband shopped with their son for stereo and computer components. (Even in this post-feminist era, this way of dividing tasks is more the rule than the exception!)

What Can You Do to Help?

Most parents find the weeks before their kid leaves trying at times. But even though you think you understand what's going on, isn't there something you can do to make this precollege summer a more pleasant time for everyone? Here are ideas that work for some families.

Try setting a date for a team effort to straighten up your kid's room. You'll probably want to get this done in any case, if only to make a little space amid the chaos. For commuter students, this process can be tremendously important; reorganizing the room they've lived in during high school helps make it clear that a new phase of life, with new responsibilities and challenges, is about to start.

Don't be discouraged by the magnitude of the task! High school papers and books, outgrown clothing that's still hanging around, and many of the bits and pieces jumbled on every surface can be stored in boxes; if you're lucky, you may be able to persuade your kid to give (or throw!) some of these things away. But even if nearly all of it ends up being kept, the process of sorting and storing can turn into a trip down memory lane for both of you. Of course, this depends on your child's willingness to set aside time for the project and also on your being able to take a fairly relaxed approach to it. If you can do that, mutual reminiscing can be a way of summing up various segments of your child's life and reliving some of the highlights.

Another thing that helps is finding someone besides yourself to give your child some advice and helpful hints about what's in store. An older sibling may have already taken on this role, and when it works, it's wonderful; advice that might sound too directive or "teacherish" coming from you sounds realistic and useful from a sister or brother who's recently been through the experience. Often a slightly older friend can provide the same kind of helpful perspective for your kid.

Some families feel it's important to put together a formal celebration. A divorced father said:

My son mostly lives with his mother, and I didn't see him often during the summer. But his stepmother and I had a party for him before he left for college. We invited his best friends and made a special meal, all the things he loves; we decorated the house with balloons and took pictures. We wanted it to be a celebration of this rite of passage.

You might also consider a joint project of some kind, if your child is amenable and you both have the time. One mother and daughter decided to make a quilt for the daughter to take to college. The mother said:

She invited friends over to quilt with us, and I invited my friends; it became a very nice thing for all of us. The quilt had pieces of clothing from all through her life, and different people embroidered on it—it was great. It also gave us something to focus on. She was getting more and more nervous as the summer went on, and I was trying to be less and less nervous, which didn't work too well. The quilt gave us something we could both be nervous about together, trying to get it finished in time. It gave us a way to deflect our nervousness.

Of course you have to plan ahead for a project like this and get started on it early, but the effort may well be worthwhile.

Pre-Orientation Programs

What about those special programs for incoming freshmen? Do they help? Many colleges now offer opportunities for incoming freshmen to spend a week at the school during the summer or to go on a wilderness trip with other freshmen before college opens for regular orientation. Lots of kids find this experience invaluable. When they get to college in the fall, they feel slightly less like fish out of water, and in many cases they've made friends they're looking forward to seeing again.

Our son went on a five-day freshman hiking trip before the regular orientation period. He was very enthusiastic about it.

It's a great idea—ten kids with two seniors spend five days together, so they really get to know each other. When we dropped him off for it, everyone was friendly and cheerful, groups meeting here and there, a very positive atmosphere. Only a small percentage of the freshmen got to do it—it was oversubscribed—so he felt very lucky.

Kids who go to college early for sports may have a similar experience. A girl who plays soccer felt that arriving two weeks early for practice with the team gave her time to find her way around the campus and to get to know her teammates pretty well. By the time other freshmen got there, she felt like an old hand.

For other kids the pre-orientation programs aren't so great. One mother said:

We made him go on the wilderness trip before orientation, but he perceived it as us making him be away from home for a week that he really wanted to spend here with his friends. It did mean that when he got to college he saw a few familiar faces the first day. But he didn't really make any friends, and it took him away from home. In retrospect, I think he shouldn't have done it.

As with everything else during this summer of see-sawing emotions, parents have to walk a narrow line, balancing their opinions about what's best for the child against the child's own wishes, and trying to figure out when to insist and when to give in gracefully.

Nonresidential colleges also provide orientation sessions for freshmen.

Our son had an overnight orientation group. He had to bring a pillow and a sleeping bag; I guess they camped out in the student lounge. They got a tour of the campus and all the obligatory lectures on sexual harassment, drinking, sex, and so on. He didn't say much about it, but I think it was helpful.

A good thing about such programs is that they draw a definite dividing line between the end of summer and the beginning of college. This forces kids, and parents, to acknowledge that college is about to happen.

To allay parental fears, some colleges now offer orientation for parents. Typically, parents and their kids spend a day or two at the college during the summer, attending separate programs. Moms and dads get a tour of the campus, hear talks on everything from drinking and date rape to study-abroad programs, and sometimes have an opportunity to stay overnight in a dorm room, whose small size and extreme decrepitude may come as a shock. Meanwhile, the kids may take placement tests, meet their advisers, and even register for courses.

Reviews on these sessions for parents are mixed. For many, they help a lot in reducing parental anxiety and fostering a sense of familiarity with the campus, which makes the prospect of September much less scary. For others, it's simply a foreshadowing of stresses to come.

My daughter and I spent three days in July at her college— orientation for both of us. She registered for her classes, and they wouldn't let the parents go with the kids to register; it was very hard for some parents to deal with that. I thought the kids would start getting to know each other, but a lot of them, including mine, didn't leave their parents' sides the whole time.

Upperclassmen, secure in their understanding of the college's mysteries, often refer to these orientation sessions patronizingly as "parent therapy." Still, if you participate in this kind of program, you'll at least have some idea of where your kid's dorm is and what the room will look like. This advance preparation can give you a comforting feeling of knowing your way around the campus.

Talking to Other Parents

For lots of families, a home-grown "support group" is the best antidote to fears and confusion. If at all possible, get together with other parents whose kids are about to start college.

> *One reason I did okay was that I talked about it a lot with my friends—you could call it anticipatory grieving. We all started envisioning what it would be like after our kids left. It was mental preparation. It's hard, but even while I was feeling sad, I could see so clearly that my daughter was ready for this next stage of her life.*

As you talk with friends, you're likely to discover that some problems and concerns are almost universal. You won't feel so bad about your child's refusal to discuss sheet and comforter colors when you find out that no one else's kid will talk about these decisions either. At the same time, you may secretly feel a lot better about your child's readiness for college when you realize that some other parents face difficulties that are worse than, or at any rate different from, your own.

Meanwhile, as your child swings between fearful self-doubt and excited anticipation, you have plenty of other things to worry about!

CHAPTER TWO

Practical Matters

Will my kid come down with measles or mono? Will he max out his new credit card and have a terrible credit rating for the rest of his life? Will she put on lots of weight because she's eating nothing but fast food and soda? How will my child survive without me to provide help?

As kids get ready to go off into the unexplored world of college, parents have lots of concerns—some large, some small, many realistic, and others unrealistic. Some of these concerns can't be resolved until much later, after the child has had time to test the waters and establish new routines and methods of coping. But others can be handled to some extent before the child's departure, which makes everyone feel a little less anxious.

You may be fortunate in having a child who is totally competent in dealing with the small but important day-to-day aspects of life. But many parents, no matter how hard they've tried to teach their high school kids to wash clothes, manage money, eat appropriately and nutritiously, and, perhaps most important, budget their time, worry that their children will be unable to cope on their own. The idea of college—a place where no one will tell their child when to get up and go to bed, what to eat, when and how much to study, and how to keep a room from becoming completely uninhabitable—fills them with dread.

I had all those regular motherly concerns, like how he'd do his laundry and whether he'd ever eat a vegetable. He's so disorganized—in high school his papers were always late, and once he got behind, it got worse and worse. I just hoped he'd be able to get himself organized once he was there. That was my biggest worry.

Parents worry about many of the same issues for kids who will be living at home. An erratic class schedule may mean that a commuter student won't eat many meals at home under your watchful eye, and once college starts, your child's increased independence is likely to extend to many new areas.

A Crash Course in Laundry

The good thing about practical concerns is that you can actually do something about them, which makes you feel better, if nothing else. Try starting with the laundry, a topic that's relatively free of emotional freight, and don't be afraid to recount some cautionary tales.

My daughter assured me she knew all about washing her clothes, but then she ran into a friend who had just finished his freshman year. He was wearing a T-shirt that had yellowish blotches all over it, and he told her his sad story—just before coming home from college, he had dumped a load of wash in the dryer and turned it on. Unfortunately it turned out that the last person to use it had left a felt-tip pen in the machine, and of course it leaked all over his clothes. She thought it was kind of funny, but not if it happened to her.

Assume that your child knows nothing and proceed down a list, beginning with everyday garb: underwear, T-shirts, socks, jeans, shorts, shirts, and so on. Discuss the dangers of mixing new dark or bright clothing with light colors (the prospect of wearing pink underwear and T-shirts for a semester focuses most kids' attention); point out the reasons, such as undissolved detergent globs, to avoid overloading the machine; and don't neglect the question of shrinkage—many college students have blithely tossed a wool sweater into the hot-water cycle or the dryer and been dismayed at the drastically smaller result.

If you feel your child has grasped the basics, you may want to move on to an advanced course in bleach and stain removal, but it's probably not necessary, at least for now. Keep in mind, too, that even a child who knows how to iron his own shirts can probably benefit from a quick refresher course.

Sleeping and Waking

Sleep is on many parents' minds, especially if they recall many "all-nighters" in their own pasts. A mother said:

> *My biggest concern for my son is that he won't get enough sleep—that was my problem in college. He needs a lot of sleep and I'm thinking, How will he manage? But what can you do? Nothing, except worry, I guess.*

She's right; there's very little you can do to ensure that your kid gets enough sleep. But most students do manage to make it through the semester despite sleep deprivation, and most of them plan to make up for lost sleep during their vacations. Does it work? More or less, and parents are often surprised by how responsibly their children behave—getting work done on time, not skipping too many classes—on insufficient sleep.

Still, it's hard for most kids to get up in time for an early class, and here you can do something eminently practical. Many college students recommend getting a clock with a very loud and long alarm; placed far enough away, it requires the sleeper to get out of bed and cross the room in order to turn it off. It's not a guarantee, but it's a big step in the right direction.

Have you been in the habit of waking your child up every morning to get to high school on time? If so, you're not alone, but you can help your son or daughter prepare for college by giving up this responsibility and letting your child take it over. Ideally you should begin hardening your heart during the second half of senior year. You may feel you have to do it gradually—many parents can't force themselves to let a kid sleep through an important test—and of course you should warn your child that you won't be waking him up anymore. But taking the consequences of being late to school a few times won't do your kid any permanent harm, and it will help him stop depending on you for this service.

Even if you don't start this weaning process until the summer, it's well worth doing as preparation for September. And it's as important for commuter students as for those who will be going away. Many students who live at home have complicated class schedules; expecting your child to get himself up in time helps him take responsibility in other aspects of his life as well.

Eating More than Junk

Food is a complicated issue, with many variations depending on your kid's circumstances and preferences. But whether she's living at home or buying a meal plan on campus, you will have considerably less influence on what she eats than you might wish. At most campus dining halls there is an enormous range of food choices, and it's possible for students to subsist on hamburgers and french fries all year long. In addition, class schedules may disrupt any chance of eating three meals a day during what parents consider

normal dining hours—not to mention the ever-present temptation to order in pizza or go out for a quick fix of fast food.

You may find, though, that your worries about your
child's eating are unfounded (or perhaps merely a substitute
for worries about other, less concrete issues).

*My daughter had a crazy class schedule her first semester,
and she's a picky eater anyway, so I was concerned that she
wouldn't eat enough. But my son went up to visit her soon
after school started, and she had some apples she'd brought
back from the dining hall to snack on that evening. She told
him the food was fine and the dining hall hours were very
flexible. I felt foolish for worrying about it, but I also felt
relieved.*

Most parents run through a list of commonsense remind-
ers before college begins: Sensible nutrition will help kids
stay healthy and alert, especially when they're short on
sleep; eating breakfast (a meal ignored by many students)
has been shown to improve mental performance throughout
the day; and too much junk food and soda are likely to
produce the dreaded first-semester weight gain known as
the Freshman Fifteen.

Breakfast is often a big issue for parents, especially if
your child already prefers sleeping later to eating a healthy
morning meal on school days. Trying to convert your kid
to your point of view on this (otherwise known as nagging!)
probably won't do much good. However, a calm discussion
may generate some reasonable alternatives that might work:
A supply of granola bars or trail mix in his room to grab
as he runs out the door to class? An arrangement to have
fresh fruit delivered to her room at regular intervals, if that's
what will entice her to eat in the mornings? At many colleges, kids can carry fruit or other portable food from the
dining hall back to their rooms to eat the next morning;
this also works for a quick lunch when classes run from
midmorning through midafternoon.

Still, it's usually best to face the fact that you've pretty much lost control of the food issue by this stage of your child's life. Plan to bring along a sack of crunchy apples or some baby carrots (which have the advantage of requiring no peeling) when you go to Parents' Weekend, and take comfort from the fact that most kids, after the first few weeks, settle into a relatively sane eating style. If you're really worried, consider sending a bottle of vitamins to school with your child.

Cars—Yes or No?

What about cars? Most students think they'd love to bring a car to college. But at residential colleges it's rarely a good idea. There's never enough parking, and if any spaces are available for first-year students, they're usually at the farthest edge of the campus. More likely a freshman's car must be parked on the street, which inevitably means a lot of time spent driving in circles looking for a space and also a lot of parking tickets. In addition, a car is simply one more thing to keep track of at a time when your kid's head is already spinning with schedules and appointments and due dates of all sorts. Fortunately, many colleges don't permit freshmen who live on campus to have cars—this is a good rule for parents to know about!

If your kid does take a car to college, be sure to find out what will be the most economical approach to insuring it. Rules and requirements vary from one insurer to the next, so it's wise to discuss the options with your insurance agent.

Commuter students are more likely to need cars; even if public transportation is available in your area, you may decide it's too inconvenient, or even too dangerous, for your child to wait for infrequent buses and to walk home from a bus stop after evening classes. But you'll want to find out all the variables in insurance requirements; in some cases it's better for you to own the car your child uses, and in other cases it may be better to register it in your child's name.

Whatever you decide, a family discussion is a good idea to make sure everyone knows who will be responsible for gas, regular maintenance, repairs, and other expenses; you may also want to talk over issues such as whether your kid's friends and classmates are allowed to drive the car and what your child should do in case there's an accident or the car is stolen. These may be questions you dealt with when your kid first began driving, but it doesn't hurt to go over them again now.

Medical and Other Help

Most colleges have lots of help available on campus for all kinds of problems. For example, you will receive plenty of information about the college health service and how to use it, and about health insurance available through the school. If your child will be covered by your health insurance instead of the college's, it's important to find out how your plan deals with students living away from home. Go over all this information with your kid a couple of times, and make sure she understands the need to carry her insurance card, from the college or from your health insurance plan, in her wallet.

Keep all this insurance and health services information handy at home. Your kid may be unable to take it all in right now, and in the information overload of the first weeks of school, she may not retain these items. But when she calls in October to say she has a sore throat, you'll know how and where to direct her for help.

It's also a good idea to discuss with your child the whole question of medical problems and what constitutes a medical emergency. Some kids tend to view everything as an emergency, while others hobble around on a broken ankle while insisting they're perfectly fine. Talk over some possi-

ble scenarios and explain who your child should call in
each case.

This discussion is especially important if your child has
a disability or medical condition that may need attention or
monitoring. Your kid's asthma, diabetes, severe allergies, or
other chronic illness can be a source of tremendous worry
in addition to all the other parental concerns you're experiencing. Take time during the summer to talk about any medical condition realistically and matter-of-factly. Try, too, to
convey your expectation that your child will be able to manage his illness on his own while making use of the assistance
that's available.

The college will no doubt send you information on other
kinds of help available to students, including the advisers
your child will be able to consult about academic and other
questions. Hang on to this information as well, so you'll
know where it is when you need it.

Money Matters

As they go off to college, most kids are likely to have more
control of, and more decisions to make about, their finances
than they've ever had before. And there are almost as many
ways of handling a college student's money as there are
families. Checking accounts, ATM cards, credit cards, and
debit cards are all options to consider. In addition, some
colleges have "savings accounts" administered by the school:
you deposit a certain amount in the account, and your child
can draw on it for any on-campus purchase, from books
to cappuccino.

Your own resources, your child's savings from gifts and
wages, and any financial aid your child will receive are the
major factors in working out a budget. Most colleges provide ballpark figures for expenses such as books and student
activities fees, which gives you a starting point, and you'll
need to allot a certain amount for initial purchases for your

child's room. For commuting students, you'll need to work out transportation expenses. After that, though, it's often hard to have any idea of how much money your child will need.

Talking to students who are upperclassmen at your kid's college can be very helpful; their parents, too, can give you ideas based on their experience. But the most important thing to do is sit down and talk frankly to your child about money. It's the rare family that doesn't find paying for a college education a stretch, and kids need to know what the ground rules will be.

> *My daughter had to get a job when she started college—it's one of the requirements of her financial aid—so she had a regular source of money coming in. We told her, "You keep the money you earn and pay for as many expenses as you can, including your phone, your books, and going out for the occasional pizza or movie. But if you see you're getting into trouble, try to give us some notice so we can work something out."*

It's common for parents to pay for tuition and room and board while kids use their own savings for spending money, and for many families this works well. But the expenses, especially at first, can come as a shock.

> *My son felt like he had so much money at the beginning, but after he bought the books for his courses, he found his funds were drastically depleted—and then came the first phone bill.*

Books for college classes are astonishingly expensive, and, though used books certainly save money, it's often impossible for kids to find secondhand copies of texts for particular classes. Many parents feel that books shouldn't be considered "expenses" in the same category as pizza, and often this makes sense. If you agree to pay for any required course materials, such as lab fees as well as books, then your

child's decisions about what to spend money on are really
his own choices, and his responsibilities. Similarly, if you
have purchased a meal plan, you can explain to your kid
that you are paying for three meals a day, and anything else
she decides to eat falls under her expenses.

For students who will be commuting to college and living at home, there may be other questions to consider. Will
your child have a job while she's going to school? If so, do
you expect her to contribute some of her earnings toward
household expenses, or will that income be her spending
money? Talk it over as a family and try to agree on a plan
that seems reasonable and possible.

It's a good idea to spell out all the financial issues as
clearly as you can. For many families, discussing money is
as difficult as talking about sex, but overcoming your reluc-
tance is important. When you let your kid know at least the
general outlines of your financial status, you acknowledge
his growing maturity and responsibility, and he's likely to
respond with a more careful approach to spending. It helps
to ask for his ideas. Do you plan to give him an allowance
every month? Discuss what expenses it should cover. Talk
about what will happen if there's an emergency: Will you
transfer money to your kid's account? Will he be listed on
your credit card so he can buy an unexpected plane ticket
home if necessary? Try to figure out what method will work
best for all of you.

Kids vary widely in their ability to manage money on
their own.

*My daughter never had a problem sticking to a budget, but
my son doesn't have the same good sense about money—he
spends it like water. I had to remind him that funds are limited
and I can only give him so much; if he wants more, he'll have
to work for it. I never had to tell my daughter that, they're
two different people. I'm afraid of credit cards for my son,
afraid he'll overspend; I don't think he knows how much
money is worth. He says he's saving for a car, but that's*

totally unrealistic. Still, my daughter says he'll become more responsible once he's actually at college—I hope so.

Bank Accounts

Many high school students have had savings accounts, but most haven't had to manage their own money. A father said:

When my daughter was going to college, we opened a checking account for her; we got the checkbook and went over what she should do and how it works. Then I put in a sum of money at the beginning of the first semester, and my ex-wife put in the same amount at the beginning of second semester. Our daughter paid her phone bill and everything else except books out of that money. It was important to me to do it that way. When I went to college, my parents gave me money each month; some months there was more and some months less, and I found it very hard to know how much I had.

Much depends on your own situation and your child's experience in handling money. One parent said, "My son is the kind of kid who hates to ask for money, so if he asks, I know he really needs it." For another, things were entirely different: "My daughter didn't do well in the beginning and went through a *lot* of money. After her phone was cut off because she couldn't pay the bill, we set up a strict budget."

Whatever you decide, you need to make sure your kid knows how the system works. It's easy to assume that a kid who seems adult in many ways knows all the details, but often he doesn't.

Our son hadn't had a checking account before and had no idea what to do—the first time he tried to deposit a check, he didn't have a deposit slip and didn't know his account number, and he was totally embarrassed and very upset. Also, he was intimidated about using his ATM card, which he had never had before; it would have been helpful if we'd practiced so he'd have known how to use it before he left.

Practicing in advance is definitely a good idea. In fact, a child who has begun using a checkbook and ATM card in high school will find coping with college expenses much easier than one who hasn't had any experience with the mechanics of banking. But it's never too late: Consider opening a checking account for your child at your bank during the summer, and encourage him to use it. This allows him to assume the responsibility for his money gradually, and you'll be available to offer advice and assistance as he gets used to the process.

You're likely to receive information about opening accounts at various banks near the college. If you open a checking account in advance, it will be ready when your child gets there. When the checkbook arrives in the mail, sit down with your child and explain how it works—how to write a check, how to keep a running tally of the account, including ATM withdrawals, and so on. For kids who haven't used a checking account before, emphasize the importance of entering debits and withdrawals every day, rather than waiting till the end of the month (or never). The "invisible" money has a way of dwindling far too fast, and kids are upset and indignant when they're charged a surprisingly high fee for overdrawing the account.

Local banks sometimes offer student accounts that don't charge for checks, but they may require that the balance doesn't go below a minimum amount; make sure your child is aware of this or similar restrictions, and also of the fees charged for using the bank's and other ATMs. If possible, shop around among the banks near campus; fees and required minimum balances may vary, and some may offer interest-bearing checking accounts.

Students at most colleges tend to use ATMs frequently, so you should talk over safety issues with your kid. Most important is the need to collect the receipt as well as the cash; leaving it lying in the machine is an invitation to unauthorized withdrawals by someone else. Suggest also that your kid try to use ATMs in well-lit and heavily trafficked locations, because isolated cash machines may attract people who prey on students. The goal is not to scare your child unnecessarily but to encourage a commonsense attitude.

Credit Cards

You may also want to discuss credit cards, which are readily available; at many colleges credit card providers set up tables so students can sign up as they wait in line to register for classes. Some parents feel that a credit card is too much for their inexperienced child to deal with in the first year or semester; others feel confident that their child is ready for this responsibility—in fact, lots of first-year students have had their own credit cards in high school.

Again, it's important to talk over the details. Make sure your child understands the penalties, in the form of very high interest charges, of not paying the credit card bill in full every month. Try getting out the calculator and asking your child to figure out the interest charges on a purchase of $200 paid off with a $15 minimum payment each month; you, as well as your kid, may be shocked to see how much the interest adds up to by the time the original charge is paid in full.

Sadly, a large number of college students max out their credit cards, mostly because they're not paying enough attention and they don't entirely understand how the charges for this kind of credit can mount up. Since credit cards are readily available to students, kids can end up with several maxed-out cards and huge debts to pay off; some drop out of college, and others risk losing their financial aid. Buying on credit is awfully tempting, for adults as well as inexperienced kids. So it's crucial to discuss it with your child, and to point out that holding on to the receipts provides an easy way of tracking what's been spent each month.

Phones

Phones at college also have to be paid for. How the phone service works varies, but many colleges leave it up to students to arrange and pay for their own phone connections directly. Since hardly a kid exists who doesn't want a phone, try to make some plans in advance. A common arrangement is for roommates to share the costs of installation and local service equally, and to pay for their own long-distance calls as listed on the monthly bills. This generally works fine, though kids are often surprised at having to figure in the tax.

They can be even more surprised at how fast the cost of long-distance calls can mount up. You might decide that you'll phone your kid instead of having him call you, so that concern about the cost won't deter him from talking to you, especially in the first few weeks or months. Collect calls are outrageously expensive, and many parents find it's cheaper to have their kid phone when it's a good time for him to talk and then to call him back, thus putting most of the charge on the parents' phone. Others install an 800 number specifically for their kid to use in calling home; you may want to consider this or ask your phone company what other options exist. In any case, it's a good idea to make sure your kid realizes that phone service will probably be one of his living expenses.

Feelings about Finances

Parents of college-bound kids are looking at big financial commitments, and it can be pretty scary to turn over any decisions about money to an eighteen-year-old. But it also can be hard to talk to your kid about the larger issues surrounding money for college. It's an emotional topic that often generates uncomfortable or unwelcome feelings.

My daughter's high school counselor pushed her to apply to very expensive schools, while we felt we could only afford a state university. It was hard; all kinds of people kept telling her, and us, "Oh, too bad you can't go somewhere else," meaning "somewhere better, and more expensive." So I feel terribly guilty that she's going to go to a state school. But meanwhile, my brother's daughter goes to a private college, and she feels guilty that he's spending all this money on her college education. So you can't win.

While some parents feel guilty that they can't afford an expensive college, and others try to avoid using their financial sacrifices as a guilt-inducing reproach to their child, still others end up feeling resentful if they believe their kid is not taking college seriously enough to warrant the money they're spending and the debts they're incurring. How much of all this should you discuss with your child? There's no answer that fits every family, though probably some discussion is desirable. Most parents want to impress upon their kid the magnitude and importance of the amount they're about to spend, without using it as a club or a sacrificial offering.

The best you can do is to discuss the financial realities with your child as openly as you can without major discomfort. Most important, make it clear that the sooner you know about any problems with money, the sooner they can be solved.

Academic Concerns

The main purpose of attending college is to get a good education—right? So a major concern on most parents' minds is how well their kids will do academically. Presumably, the admissions staff wouldn't have accepted your child if they didn't think she'd be able to succeed in her courses. But most parents, and most kids, can't help worrying.

The temptation is almost overpowering to sit your kid down for a lecture that will include admonitions to get organized, work hard, stick to a schedule, and avoid procrastinating. And once you've said all that, you add the warning that failure to get good grades will probably result in losing financial aid.

This nearly universal lecture is fine, as long as you realize that in some ways it's being delivered too late: at this point you're no longer in charge, and it's up to your kid to make these choices (though parents often wonder if their kid really understands the possible consequences). If your child breezed through high school, getting good grades without much effort, you may worry about how he'll do when all the other freshmen were at the top of their high school class, too.

There's no way to eliminate these concerns, but you can try to ensure that you don't send an unintended message. It's fine to convey your expectation that your kid will work hard and be responsible about going to class and doing the required work. Be careful, though, about implying that this hard work will inevitably lead to his getting straight A's; in the real world of college, it may not. If fabulous grades result, that's great; but if they don't, his hard work will have led to his learning a great deal, and that's great, too. Your kid will feel less pressured if you make it clear that your expectations apply to his behavior rather than his grades.

Be cautious also about giving your child the impression that you expect good grades as "payment" for the money you're shelling out for college. One danger here is that your child will feel she must take safe courses—ones she'll do well in but that won't challenge her or offer the new horizons that are part of the purpose of going to college. If you can get across your expectation that your child will get the most she can from her college experience, she's likely to do her best to fulfill it.

A related concern for parents is whether their child's college education will be "worth it." Will it prepare him for getting a job? They have nightmare visions of four years spent on "useless" courses in rap music and ancient Icelandic sagas, at the end of which their kid, though educated, will be unemployable.

The reality is that many, and perhaps most, students entering college don't know what they want to major in or what kind of career they want after college. Some kids have a plan; if they know they want to be doctors or teachers or engineers, they'll have a schedule of required courses. But even kids who have things mapped out—expecting to major in economics or elementary education or psychology, for instance—often change their minds. And that's not such a bad thing when you think about it. A college administrator says, "Kids today are far less likely to stay in the same job or even the same profession for their whole working lives than they were thirty years ago. We have to recognize that reality and help them prepare for it with an education that avoids a too-narrow focus."

Yet young people feel tremendous pressure to take courses that will lead to a particular career.

I want my son to take courses that will be practical in terms of an occupation when he leaves college. He's taking a lot of art courses, and artists don't make much money.

Such feelings are understandable; after all, we all want our children to be comfortable in life. But the emphasis on college as mainly a ladder to a job is deplored by most educators. They prefer an emphasis on learning to think clearly and deeply, and on taking courses that engage a student's passionate enthusiasm. Learning how to learn, to think, and to work hard has the added benefit of preparing a student for an unpredictable future job market that will require flexibility and an active mind.

You'll probably be thinking about all this as you and your child look at the course catalog, the requirements for graduation, and the multitude of electives available for first-year students. Some kids welcome help from their parents in choosing what to take, and at some schools the process isn't easy.

> *We sat down with my daughter for three or four hours, trying to figure out the core curriculum stuff and the requirements. It was like a Chinese puzzle where you say, Oh, no, if I do this, then I can't do that, and you have to start over. She could never have done it by herself—every parent at the school says the same thing.*

But many kids want to be independent as they begin this phase of their academic career; they are happy to discuss the options and listen to advice, but then they make their own choices. Still others don't even want to talk about it.

> *With my older son, my input was the kiss of death—a sure way to make him not take a course I thought would be good. So with my younger son I kept my mouth shut and let him choose.*

Still, there are a few ways you can help in this confusing and anxiety-producing process. If it's possible for your child to talk to a student who is already attending the college, he may get useful firsthand information about teachers and courses.

> *We had some general discussion about what kind of courses my son should take; as a possible math major, he'll probably need serious math courses. But I also told him that the most important thing is to find out what the professor is like; I told him to ask older students, because you don't get that kind of information from the college catalog.*

Some colleges, especially those where kids must register for courses before they arrive on campus, have a student-run hot line with advice about courses; encourage your child to make use of it. Also, make sure your kid realizes that freshmen don't always get into the courses they want, so it's a good idea to have several alternate choices in mind. And, depending on your child, you may want to suggest that five mornings of eight o'clock classes could be a difficult commitment to stick with for a night owl, or a potential night owl.

You still may worry that your child will spend four years analyzing the work of minor twelfth-century poets and end up with neither a well-rounded education nor a marketable skill. But as you discuss the courses she will take the first year, try to encourage her to look for electives in subjects she really wants to learn about. It's one way to help foster the intellectual excitement you hope she'll discover.

If you think your kid is choosing too many courses that are too difficult, you may want to suggest spreading them out over two semesters instead of taking them all right away. You don't want to imply that you think she can't do the work, but you can point out the wisdom of walking into the deep water slowly so she won't get in over her head.

If the opportunity presents itself, you may want to talk with your child about the ways that college courses are likely to differ from high school classes. For most students college courses will be harder, with more reading on a more sophisticated level than they are used to. In addition, college professors provide considerably less day-to-day supervision than most high school teachers do, so it's very easy for kids to fall behind in their work, and then even all-night cramming before an exam doesn't undo the damage.

A possible preventive measure is a course in study skills. Many colleges offer these to students who are having academic difficulties, but it may be more useful to take one in advance, perhaps over the summer. Even if your child resists the idea at first, he may come to see the potential value of learning techniques for studying more efficiently, and be more likely to seek this kind of help at college before he gets overwhelmed.

CHAPTER THREE

Parental Anxieties: Social and Emotional Issues

What if her roommate parties all the time and has boys sleep over in the room? Will he feel pressured to choose between drinking himself into a stupor or being branded as a geek? Will she feel lost in the crowd on a huge campus, or limited and bored on a small one? Will he find lifelong friends? Will she be safe?

In any random sample, nine out of ten parents would say their main concerns about college revolve around social and emotional issues. Sending your child into an entirely new situation in which you have little or no role to play means you have no control over how things go. You can't ban alcohol from the birthday party, you can't set the curfew and the penalty for violating it, you can't even monitor the TV programs. When asked what they worry about, above and beyond financial and academic questions, most parents say things like "I just hope he'll be happy and have a good experience" or "My main concern is that she be comfortable there and make friends."

> *I hoped she would find a niche, people she would want to be with. She was leaving a small group of close friends she'd been with all her life. I hoped she'd find that again, hoped she'd get along with her roommates and make some good friends.*

Yet making new friends isn't easy at any stage of life. A kid who goes to school near home probably knows at least a few fellow students, but he won't necessarily see much of them; they're likely to be in different classes, on different schedules, and their paths may not cross very often. A child who's going away to school is even less likely to have a group of good friends available; you may feel that she's going to be dropped into a pond without a boat or even a life jacket. This can be a thrill for a kid, but it can also be a pretty scary jump off a cliff.

Some see the prospect of a new social milieu as a wonderful adventure, and their parents feel little concern on that score.

She was looking forward to entering a strange environment where she didn't know a soul—she just knew she was going to meet a lot of great kids, and she did.

For other kids, however, parents feel fearful.

I felt my son was socially immature and would have a rough time dealing with new people in a relaxed way. I thought about how unskilled he was socially, like a babe in the woods— it filled me with worry and sadness.

Another parent said:

It was just like when she started nursery school—I wanted her to make friends and have a great time, but it was something I couldn't do anything about, I couldn't do it for her.

Of course there are various aspects of the college social scene that may give you pause. Your child will be on his own in an unfamiliar place. One mother said:

I've heard there is a very active social life at my son's college. I'm concerned that he not get so caught up in it that he doesn't have time to study, but that he not be left out of it, either.

This comment neatly sums up two different concerns. On one hand, parents hope their kid will be able to manage all the freedom and will cling to the rules and values he's been brought up with; on the other hand, they hope their child will develop satisfying social relationships and have a lot of fun. And at the same time parents know that there's not a great deal they can do to influence their child's social experience at college.

Roommates

My main concern was the roommate situation. My own college roommate was as different from me in every way as possible. Things eventually worked out, but it was hard for me.

Often parents' first question on social matters is about roommates. Most colleges send incoming students a roommate questionnaire; in addition to questions about such things as tastes in music, late-night and early-morning waking and sleeping, and levels of tolerance for mess, it may ask for the name of a student's preferred roommate. This is the time for your kid to decide whether to room with a friend or not.

For a freshman, the safety of rooming with someone he already knows is tempting, but there are a few negatives to discuss with your child before he says yes. Rooming with a good friend can prevent a kid from branching out and exploring the wide range of possible new friends at college; there's a risk of becoming cocooned and a bit isolated.

Perhaps more important, a kid who does branch out and form new relationships while rooming with a friend from home often finds that the bond with his old friend/room-

mate becomes strained, even broken, especially if the roommate is more fearful about seeking new companions. Such a
kid may then feel guilty about leaving his old friend behind
socially, annoyed at his buddy's need to hold on to him
with an iron grasp, and saddened at the possible loss of a
valued friendship. This scenario is difficult and distressing
for anyone to go through, but it occurs often enough that
your child should consider the question carefully.

Do you hope to influence your child's choices about
roommates, even if she's not planning to room with a
friend? Of course you do, in a sense; one mother said, "I
wanted her to have a good roommate; you hear such scary
stories about strange people." But at most colleges the questionnaire is the only way you or your child can influence
roommate assignments, and it's not useful to shade the truth
in the answers. For your kid, saying she goes to bed early,
gets up at the crack of dawn, and listens only to Beethoven,
when in reality she stays up late and sleeps till noon whenever possible and has her radio permanently tuned to classic
rock, probably won't result in a happy roommate combination. On the other hand, it might: A father said, "My son is
very different from his roommate, but he sees that as a positive, not a negative." Still, it's best to give the roommate
assigners accurate information to work with.

Some parents try to influence their children's roommate
choices in other ways, making racial and ethnic preferences
paramount or demanding a roommate who is guaranteed
not to smoke, drink, party, or stay up late. This is not a
good idea. Apart from the fact that your kid will be able to
find students who drink and party no matter what her
roommate is like, such demands make it clear that you intend to impose your own views and control your child's life
from afar and that you don't have confidence in her ability
to make appropriate decisions. This doesn't help your child
begin a life away from you.

But some kids do become anxious in advance—what if
my roommate doesn't like me or we really don't get along?

If your kid seems worried about this possibility, reassure him that changing roommates is usually possible if they are truly incompatible; more important, if this happens to him, it isn't a failure on his part, or the roommate's part. College staff are not infallible, and some personality combinations just don't work.

Take a look at the roommate questionnaire and talk over the questions with your child if he wants to, but then let it alone and hope for the best. Most students manage to get along with their roommates without undue stress, and a few find lifelong friends.

Safety on Campus

At all but the most bucolic campuses, safety is unfortunately a bigger issue than it used to be, partly because most students no longer have curfews and many college libraries are open late or even all night. Your child's college will no doubt send you information about safety on campus and in the surrounding area, and this can be quite reassuring.

I had no concerns about security. I was very impressed; they have all these safety systems, escorts to walk you home if it's late, and blue lights to go to and press a button if you need help.

Still, especially for colleges in urban areas, safety is something you'll probably want to discuss with your child.

It's a self-contained campus but it borders a rough area where there have been incidents. We talked about it, and I gave her cautions: You don't go out at night by yourself, only with someone else; you don't walk on narrow, isolated streets by yourself; mostly common-sense kinds of things. I didn't want to make her paranoid, but you do have to be aware.

Though parents tend to worry more about girls, boys, too, can benefit from conversations about being street-smart and using good sense.

My son was walking late at night with his roommate at the edge of campus, and a group of high school boys from town approached them. One of them made a comment, my son made a comment, and the next thing was that these kids sprayed Mace in their faces. They were okay, but I was in a panic that my son's eyes might have been damaged. I realized that coming from a quiet suburban area, he was unprepared for this kind of confrontation and hadn't worked out a way to handle it.

Part of the problem, of course, is the feeling of most teenagers that they are invincible and nothing bad will happen to them. Meanwhile, from a parental point of view, you worry that you won't know what time your child gets home at night or even where he goes when he's out—and you wonder if anyone on campus will know where he is. You want to prepare your child for the possibilities, but at the same time, you don't want to make him unnecessarily fearful. Keep your warnings realistic and present them calmly; remember, too, that once on campus your kid will pick up cues from other students and advisers about what is and isn't safe.

If your child is going to college far away from home, a visit to the campus and the city beforehand can be helpful in giving both you and your kid a sense of how to get around in a new place. For commuter students, too, especially those who will take public transportation to school, a practice run is useful.

After our daughter was accepted, we went to see the school. We weren't going to be able to take her there in September; she would have to go by train to the center city and then switch to a commuter train to the suburb where the college is. So we walked through the main station in the city to see where to get the commuter train; then we took that train to the college. On the way we were figuring out what landmarks she should watch for so she'd know where to get off. The conductor could see she was a newcomer, and he was very nice, talking to her about how often the trains run and how she could make sure she was on a local and not an express. Afterwards we all felt better, knowing that she had practiced and wouldn't get lost.

It's helpful to talk with a student who attends your child's college or has recently graduated. Some of today's campus realities may come as a shock, especially at big universities or those in urban areas. On a parent-orientation tour of one large campus, a father asked about safety problems and was dismayed at the student guide's reply:

It's pretty safe on campus, but you do have to pay attention— in the library, for example. When you go to the bathroom, you have to take your books with you. Otherwise, when you come back, they'll be gone—people can sell them for a lot of money. Even your class notes might be gone if it's right before midterms or finals and somebody needs to get caught up.

It can be distressing to realize that college may not be the harmonious bower of learning you envision for your kid. Perhaps you recall leaving your books on the library table while you spent an hour over coffee and never bothering to lock the door of your room during your own college days. But it's important for your child to be aware of the realities he may face, even in the dorm.

About ten one morning my son was dozing, about to get up for class. He heard the door of his room open and thought his roommate had come back for something, but when he turned over and opened his eyes he saw a total stranger just going out the door. My son jumped out of bed only to discover that

his wallet and watch had been stolen from the top of his desk.
Who would have imagined that you'd have to lock your door
even when you're sleeping in your room?

It's unfortunate but true that on many campuses it's risky
to leave doors open and valuables in plain sight. Still,
though parents may find them upsetting, kids do get used
to whatever conditions prevail at their college and learn to
take precautions.

Racial and Ethnic Tensions

As you anticipate sending your kid onto a campus full of
strangers, you can't help wondering what the other students
will be like. One thing many parents find themselves worrying about is the question of racial and class divisions. Will
your child feel out of place if he represents any kind of
minority—racial, ethnic, religious, or financial—on campus?
Will he be able to find others like himself so he won't feel
alone? Will he have a better and richer experience if he tries
not to stick with people just like him?

Parents, as well as kids, have varying views on these
questions, and they are definitely important topics to discuss
as a family. Colleges, too, have differing policies on these
delicate matters; at every college officials hope to make all
their students feel equally comfortable and accepted, but
what's politically correct at one school may be rejected at
another. And some policies can backfire, alienating the very
kids they're intended to welcome.

At the orientation weekend in the spring they paired kids with
sophomores to stay overnight and get a taste of the college.
Both my son and I got very annoyed because they seemed to
pair the black kids only with other black kids. That bothered
us because it's not where we're coming from—we have friends

of all races and backgrounds, and I expect, and hope, my son
will meet many kinds of people at college.

For other families, though, staying overnight with a student from a similar background is a reassuring experience that can provide firsthand, realistic advice about the social scene from one who's already there.

On some campuses there is a good deal of "self-segregation." A student said:

> *Lots of people at my school stick to their own groups. At lunch you see a table of blacks in the cafeteria, a table of South Asians, maybe a table of Koreans or Chinese. But it's not just ethnic. You see a table of football players, a table of fraternity brothers, they stick together, too.*

Such self-segregation seems to be encouraged at some colleges, where students may live in black dorms or Asian dorms, as well as dorms devoted to other kinds of groups.

Is self-segregation a good idea? Only you and your child can decide, based on your family's beliefs, circumstances, and comfort level in various settings. How important will it be for your child to feel part of a group? It can provide lots of support and a strong sense of belonging, which are valuable, especially in the first uncertain days and weeks. But it can also be quite isolating, cutting a kid off from other kinds of experiences and people.

Many students, particularly those who have grown up in mixed communities, resent being identified by the college primarily as minority-group representatives. A freshman remembered:

> *During orientation the college had a lunch for minority parents and kids. My parents thought it was a nice group of people, and my mom said it was very "comfortable." But I think it was more comfortable for the parents than for the kids. We already knew we were minorities, they brought us to*

school early for that reason, they said we "needed more time to adjust." That made me angry, as if we wouldn't be able to make it without special help.

A parent said:

My daughter went on a weekend for accepted students to see if she wanted to go to that college. They had a "pajama party" for minority kids, so there were a few Latinas, a few blacks, a few South Asians, a few Chinese, and so on. They all formed their own groups as soon as they arrived. She didn't want to sit with only other Latinas, she thought that was stupid, but the blacks and the Chinese and others didn't welcome her in their groups. She was upset, and it made her decide not to go to that school.

As you talk about these issues with your child, try to emphasize that decisions needn't be made immediately. Kids shouldn't feel forced by others to define themselves, though such pressure is often present. A Chinese-American student said:

In high school I didn't have any close friends who were Chinese, but at college I got friendly with two girls. After a while they said, "You have to be friends with only us or not at all; you have to choose between us and your non-Chinese friends." I told them, "Forget it, I don't live in China, if you're making me choose that's the end of it." I didn't even join the Chinese club, just for that reason.

But another student remembered how good it felt to be part of a large group of African-Americans after having been one of only two in a mostly white high school.

Sometimes it feels like a no-win situation for everyone: Members of the minority group resent it if a kid doesn't do everything with them, while nonmembers resent the group's exclusiveness, seeing it as unfriendliness. But over time most students work things out in a way that's comfortable for them.

Of course, much depends on how large the various minority populations are at your child's college. There's no denying that a kid who's one of a small minority can feel very lonely. One student said, "The worst time was Yom Kippur—I was one of about twelve Jews on campus, and everybody kept asking, 'How come you're not eating?' "

What about racism on campus? No one likes to think about this, but just as in the rest of the world, it can happen anywhere. Certainly you'll want to encourage your child to report any overtly racist behavior immediately. For minor incidents—thoughtless jokes or offensive comments—it's a good idea to discuss appropriate responses with your kid before he leaves home. Everyone draws his or her own line between what can and should be ignored and what ought to be confronted, and it's helpful to talk this over openly beforehand. Be realistic, but try not to set up negative expectations about the college; most of them work hard to eliminate racism from their campuses, and most offer both sympathy and help to any student who experiences racist behavior from others.

Sex, Drugs, and Drinking

Even after you convince yourself that like most kids, yours will adjust well and make new friends at college, you'll probably come up with other things to worry about. There are far fewer rules on today's college campuses than on those of yesteryear, and this can be hard for parents to get used to. Will your kid be able to manage all this freedom?

Alcohol, drugs, and sex are on most parents' minds as their children get ready to leave for college. A mother said, "You talk to your kid about unprotected sex, date rape, drugs, and alcohol, and then you keep your fingers crossed."

Another recalled her worries during her son's first semester at college:

> *He got caught up in a lot of behavior we didn't like. I think there was a lot of peer pressure, and he was intrigued with marijuana. Then he had a bad experience and stayed away from it after that. He told us about it—I was glad he talked to us, but I still didn't feel happy about what he'd been doing.*

Away from home, there will be no parental rules to provide an easy way for a kid to say no; he'll have to make his own decisions now. A parent said:

> *I worry about both alcohol and drugs because he'll be in an unsupervised environment and the place has a reputation as a party school. You see your kids every day when they're home, but you don't when they're at school, so you don't know what's happening.*

Commuter students, even though they're living at home, are likely to expect much more freedom from parental rules than they had during the high school years. Be prepared for strong resistance if you attempt to establish, or continue, a curfew! Probably all the old rules will be subject to renegotiation, and this may make you feel a bit uneasy.

> *We live in a suburban area, and my son is going to college way downtown in the city. He commutes by train every day. He's met a lot of kids that he likes, and one Friday he called to say they were going out and then he was spending the night at one of the friend's homes. We hadn't said he couldn't do that, and I know he can't be a hermit without any social life, but it made me extremely nervous—I've never laid eyes on any of these kids, and the one he was staying with lives way out on the west side of the city, which is not the safest neighborhood. And I had no idea what he would be doing that night, so I was picturing an out-of-control orgy with various*

illegal substances. I felt he was drifting into dangerous waters and I didn't know how to throw him a lifeline.

Sex is even more difficult than drinking and drugs to discuss with your child; there are fewer outside guidelines to hold onto. After all, for anyone under 21 drinking is against the law, and illegal drugs are obviously illegal. But few such laws govern sexual behavior, and both parents' and students' attitudes about it range from extreme permissiveness to strict insistence on complete abstention, with many variations in between.

No matter where they stand on sexual issues, most parents admit to fears that go beyond safety issues like date rape and sexually transmitted diseases (which are discussed during orientation at nearly every college in the country). Parents worry that their child will be hurt if a partner takes a sexual relationship less seriously than he or she does; they fear that the temptation to indulge in one-night-stand-style sex will undermine the principles they've tried to instill in their kid; they fret about what problems a rule-less dormitory environment will pose for their son or daughter. One mother said:

> *One of the things I discussed with my daughter before she left was what if her roommate had boyfriends stay overnight? My daughter said she would not put up with it. I was glad she felt that way, but I worried that it could be very awkward and difficult for her if this happened.*

It's tempting for parents to hope that somehow or other their child will be able to avoid dealing with any of these problem areas—but it's not realistic. Underage drinking, illegal drug use, and sexual activity are commonplace on most college campuses, and neither parents nor college administrators are likely to change that fact. Actually, alcohol, drugs, and sex are widely available in most high schools today. Most parents know this, though they, along with high school administrators, often persuade themselves to deny it—partly as a way to avoid dealing with uncomfortable issues.

One way to look at the whole question of alcohol, drugs, and sex in college is to consider it an opportunity for necessary growth. Facing and dealing with challenges and new situations is an important way kids learn and develop. If they never have a chance to handle a problem on their own, this stage in the maturing process is postponed.

Even so, parents rightly see these as serious matters. They can't help fearing that away from their watchful eyes, their children will be unable to make sensible decisions about these adult temptations. In addition to the moral questions involved, parents' worries include sexually transmitted diseases and designer drugs, along with such obvious dangers as drunk driving.

Still another fear for some parents, and one that is often harder to discuss with a child or to admit to oneself, involves the question of homosexuality on campus. At almost all colleges, there will be gay and lesbian students. Perhaps the most common fear for parents is that their child will be paired with a roommate who is homosexual; others may unconsciously fear, without acknowledging it to themselves in words, that their child may be encouraged to come out as a gay or lesbian while at college; still others are afraid that a child who has already come out will face prejudice and perhaps outright hostility from other students.

The concept of homosexuality at college is terrifying to some parents, somewhat discomforting to a large group, and entirely unimportant to others. If the prospect distresses you, it may help to keep a few things in mind:

• Your child is unlikely to be seduced by a homosexual roommate or dormmate; just as in heterosexual seductions, it takes two interested parties to get things started.

• Room changes are usually possible after a specified trial period (perhaps a month or so) if it's clear that roommates can't stand each other. Remember, though, that many kids who start out with doubts and suspicions end up feeling they can tolerate, or even become friends with, a roommate different from themselves for a semester or two.

• In many cases, parents get far more upset about this issue than their kids do, which means it's a good idea to stop and think things over before storming into the dean's office.

• Appearances and stereotypes can be misleading; don't leap to conclusions without making sure of your facts.

• The college years are a time of experimentation in many directions. A try-out of homosexuality or bisexuality at this stage doesn't always determine the path taken in later life. At the same time, for the kid who comes out while at college, the campus may provide a social environment that's more supportive and accepting than anything available back home.

So what can you do to help? Make time to talk about these things, to explain (even if it's for the zillionth time) your own values and beliefs. Your child needs to know where you stand on these questions; he also needs to know that you trust him and have confidence in his ability to make decisions about his life; and he needs to know that you are available to provide help, advice, and encouragement at any time. A divorced mother said:

> I didn't deal with the drinking question as a disciplinary matter, but I talked to my kid about the seriousness of it. His father and I are together on that; we discussed it and agreed on that approach.

In discussing these difficult issues, it works best to avoid preaching and to convey your expectations of your child in a nonconfrontational way. Yet this can be extremely hard to do. Parents often feel as if this is their last chance to influence their child's behavior and to set him on the right path, and their anxiety can make them sound dictatorial.

Try not to fall into this trap, and plan to have this conversation more than once, starting as early as you can. Kids often act as if they don't want to hear anything you have to say about these matters and can't wait to end the discussion and get away. But kids are worried about their ability to cope with the risky lifestyle questions they're likely to face at college. Under the bravado, they're usually listening, and they do remember what you say.

For your part, it's important to recognize that your child has already been exposed to these questions and may be less naïve or inexperienced than you think. Beyond providing advice and an example, as you have throughout your kid's whole life, there's not much you can do about these dangerous behaviors. It's hard to accept this, but the ideal is a balance between trusting your kid to be sensible and being ready to offer advice and help if needed.

Communication

In the rush to get ready to go to college, and then in the overwhelming newness of the first few weeks, kids may not leave much time for communicating with their parents. Parents, too, may let their preoccupation with the details prevent them from talking with their child about the important things, like finances and academics as well as social behavior. But without such conversations, parents and kids may part with different assumptions about what's expected on both sides, and the gap may simply get wider. Take time to talk about these issues, even at the risk of repeating yourself, and try to make your expectations clear to yourself and to your child.

You'll want genuine communication to continue after your kid is at college, so make this expectation clear, too. Even if he or she doesn't admit it, keeping the lines open is enormously important as new students feel their way in their new setting. Let your kid take control of things to some extent, deciding whether phone calls or e-mail or old-fashioned letters will work best. But make sure your kid knows that you'll be in touch frequently—the corollary is that he or she can reach out to you whenever the need arises.

Unspoken Fears

Finally, after you've worried about all these various topics, you may find there's a deeper, sometimes unspoken and unacknowledged concern. One parent put it this way:

> When my daughter went to school, of course I had the regular worries: Will she be happy, will she be able to do the work at a level she'll be happy with, will she find friends who will appreciate her? And the first time she drove home, I was worried she'd be in a car crash.
>
> But besides all this, I had an underlying worry: Will my kid care about us and the life we've had together, or will she abandon everything that matters to us, the way we've brought her up? These doubts aren't rational, but they're there.

A similar concern is felt by nearly all parents. They're excited and proud as their child takes the first step into a new life, but they're also sad: They feel that in some ways they are losing their child and losing their family as it has been up to now. They feel they will lose the powerful influence and the control they've had in their child's life.

The litany of losses can be devastating and a little frightening. Yet at the same time it's exhilarating to see your kid poised to take off into the unknown. Just as your child is swinging back and forth between fear and eager excitement, you may find yourself bouncing between two opposite poles—way down one day and way up the next.

It helps to take a step back and try to look at the bigger

picture. You're not the only parent who feels this way; it's normal and expected. But you can try to avoid making your child's emotional state more difficult. As one parent said, "You feel so much anxiety at the beginning, but you try not to communicate it to your kid." You don't have to hide your feelings completely (you probably can't anyway), but a little enforced calm from time to time will help everyone. Take a walk, go to a movie, talk to a friend whose child is also about to go to college—do whatever works to lessen the tension and put things in as much perspective as you can.

CHAPTER FOUR

Packing and Preparing

The day of departure is approaching fast, and you have to get your kid packed and ready to go. It sounds pretty straightforward, but often it's not. The act of packing seems to make the impending farewell feel real, almost for the first time. Emotions rise to the surface, and the whole process can easily become a magnet for tension and conflict, at exactly the time when you'd like all the family interactions to be perfect.

Packing Styles

Just as kids vary in every other way, they have different packing styles. The kind of kid who has things planned and organized well in advance can seem a little compulsive.

> *My daughter took charge of her own packing. She had lists, and her lists had lists. She started very early—maybe it was part of the process of leaving and saying good-bye. She shopped for bedding and towels bit by bit and made piles of different categories in her room. Her foot locker was in her room all summer, gradually filling up.*

On the other hand, kids who refuse to start packing until the very last minute can drive their parents to distraction.

> *My son didn't pack until the night before we left, and then he stuffed everything in plastic garbage bags without any plan or system. He was still taking his laundry out of the dryer as we got in the car the next morning.*

The last-minute packers are often the same kids who let their parents (usually mothers) do much of the preparation. A mother recalled:

> *I packed—he had nothing to do with the process from start to finish. I had bought all his sheets and things, and I packed those, since he wouldn't even look at them. But I made him at least sit there in the room while I packed his actual clothes. It was frustrating—he refused to express any opinion on what should go with him and what should stay.*

It may appear that a child who has everything folded and packed weeks in advance can't wait to get going on the college experience, while the one who puts off getting ready is reluctant to leave the safe, secure nest of home. This isn't necessarily the case. Throwing things together at the last minute may indicate supreme self-confidence about what's coming, while stretching the process of getting packed and organized over several days or weeks can be a way of combatting fears; obsessing about practical questions like how many sweatshirts to take leaves less mental energy and time to worry about the larger issues. One mother said:

> *My daughter was completely preoccupied with how many sheets and towels she should take to college. I was thinking, "My kid is leaving home forever, and life is taken up with minutiae."*

In fact, parents may find themselves behaving the same way. One mother warned, "Start making lists early; be organized." Another said, "I started shopping in June, and it helped me. Checking off stuff on a list made me feel reassured that it would all get done." Taking over the packing, at least to some extent, is a way of relieving the stress of your kid's upcoming departure; it gives you something concrete and useful to do, provides the illusory sense that you're in control of things, and keeps you from thinking too much about how you're feeling.

Whatever your kid's style, you can take comfort in knowing you have plenty of company. And the general opinion among observers, though perhaps politically incorrect, is that packing behavior tends to be gender-linked: Most girls plan, most boys postpone.

The amount of stuff kids take to college also differs greatly, and this seems to have nothing to do with gender. Here is one parent's account:

> My son took everything he owned to school—his room is an empty shell. He took every shred of clothing, sports stuff like a football and a Frisbee, a quilt, sheets, pillows, a phone, photos of his friends and his girlfriend, his CDs and tapes and a boombox, his desk chair, and a refrigerator. He took everything.

This isn't unusual. Another parent said:

> My daughter tends to travel with everything—the van was packed to the doors, there was no place left to sit. She wanted her books, she took her collection of porcelain dolls and her stuffed animals, her computer, her writing materials because she likes to write. Plus there was bedding and clothes and tapes and CDs, her tape player and her radio—her entire world.

Dormitory rooms are small and storage space is minimal, so it's a good idea to encourage taking less rather than more. Still, try not to be upset if your child wants to take "too much" stuff to college. Many kids need the security of taking their home with them; as time goes on and they begin to feel more comfortable in the new environment, they may well bring the excess items back. And what seems like too much to you may look like the bare necessities to your child; it's typical for kids to take enough toiletries (shampoo, toothpaste, soap, etc.) to last the full four years. Furthermore, in some cases your child's instincts may be right on target.

> *My daughter packed four long dresses to take to college. I couldn't believe it—my college days were spent in jeans and sandals. I told her it was idiotic to take the formal gowns: She'd never use them and they'd take up valuable closet space. But when she came home at Thanksgiving, she had already worn all four dresses at least once.*

Another mother had an entirely different experience:

> *Our only fights were about packing. Every time I suggested something I thought she needed, she said, "I don't need it, leave me alone." She had two towels, and my neighbor said she'd need more, in case she wanted to spread out a sweater to dry, but my daughter said, "What am I going to do with all these towels, I don't need them." I think she was the only girl going away to college who didn't want to buy anything. Everything I suggested, she didn't need, and she thought I was being stupid to suggest it.*

Although this kind of minimalist packing is the opposite of the take-everything-I-own method, both may be expressions of the same fears. Taking as little as possible to college may be a way of saying "I don't know if I'm ready to leave home, and I want to make it easy to come back." In a few weeks such a kid will probably be eager to augment her furnishings and make her room at college her own.

What to Pack

So how does your child figure out what to pack? Your kid's college may supply a list of recommended items (and of items that are prohibited); this list should also tell you whether the dorm beds require extra-long sheets, which is important to know before you buy. In addition, lists left over from when your child went to sleepaway camp can be useful; newspapers and magazines often run late-summer articles on furnishing dorm rooms; and many stores that sell bedding and furnishings make up lists of what college-bound kids need. Of course, lists from stores should be viewed with a slightly skeptical eye; they want to sell you as much stuff as they can. And magazine articles sometimes seem a bit remote from reality—most kids don't take over-stuffed armchairs to college, at least not in their first semester. Still, the lists can remind you of items or whole categories you've forgotten.

You may think your child already owns nearly everything he'll need at college, but most parents end up purchasing a surprising number of "necessities."

I was amazed at how much I had to buy before my son left for college, and at how much it cost. Sheets, blankets, pillows, storage crates, lamps, a new winter jacket—it all adds up. And then he chipped in with his five roommates for a couch.

As you and your kid begin to consider what's essential to take to college, keep in mind that in dorm rooms things can easily get damaged or, unfortunately, stolen. It's a good idea to leave valuable small items (such as good jewelry, expensive watches, fragile ornaments, and irreplaceable keepsakes) at home. Some students advise against laptop computers because they are so vulnerable to theft. In any case, sturdy and inexpensive are the watchwords for anything you have to buy; even if that area rug actually lasts for four years, chances are you'll want to throw it out when your kid graduates.

You and your child may disagree about what's essential and what's not. For example, many parents feel a TV in the dorm room is an unnecessary distraction from studying, while kids tend to see it as a basic essential of life. Try pointing out that there won't be much room for a TV in a typical dorm room and (if true) that your child tends to find it hard to turn the TV off and settle down to working. If nothing else, perhaps you can agree that at least the first semester will be TV-less. However, be prepared to discover that every other room on your child's floor is equipped with a TV as well as other forms of entertainment.

A major question for parents is whether their child will need a computer, and whether they can afford one. Many kids find it's not necessary to have their own computer; nearly every college has a computer center where students can go to write and print their papers and do other kinds of computer work. Others, though, think it's easier to have a computer in their room; lots of roommates end up sharing one computer setup. College stores often offer helpful advice about the campuswide network and what machines fit into it well; they may also have excellent prices. If you think your kid will want or need a personal computer, do some comparison shopping, read the informational literature about the college's system, and consider using graduation gift money toward this major purchase.

An excellent source of information about what to pack is an older student who's attending your child's college. He or she can advise your child about whether dress-up clothes are ever needed and whether dorms tend to be overheated or freezing cold. A third-year student at a school in the Northeast told an incoming freshman:

Seriously, just relax. Don't overpack; the things you don't use or wear at home you're not about to start wearing at school.

*All you need is jeans and socks and flannel shirts—and aspirin
and Pepto-Bismol for those big party nights.*

This last comment may make you wince, but it's a good
reminder that the family medicine cabinet won't be available
to your kid. You may want to add items like Band-Aids,
cough drops, and over-the-counter painkillers to your list.

Before you pack up any appliances, encourage your child
to telephone her roommate(s) and discuss who will bring
what. (This is also a chance to talk about coordinating colors
of quilts, etc., for kids to whom such decorating questions will
matter.) Items to parcel out among the roommates might include a refrigerator, TV, VCR, phone, answering machine,
iron, and audio equipment. Many colleges don't permit cooking of any kind in the dorm, but some allow popcorn poppers,
hot pots, and toaster or microwave ovens. These, too, are best
shared—it's hard to find space for one, let alone two.

Some parents worry if they can't afford to equip their
child with everything he or she could possibly need. Will a
wealthier roommate make their kid feel at a disadvantage?
Certainly our society places a good deal of emphasis on
material possessions, and many kids expect to get all sorts
of things just for the asking. However, college attitudes differ widely about the importance of material things, and
many students find that differences in income level are
mostly irrelevant to their friends. In any case, a student who
can't afford her own computer or a vast wardrobe of clothes
will certainly not be the only one in that position.

One Mom's Recollection

Here is one mother's description of her daughter's packing
for a northern midwestern college:

*Items for the room: three sets of extra-long sheets (I think
that's one set too many), plus towels, quilt, pillows, blanket,*

and plastic stacking storage shelves. She went shopping at the discount drugstore for bathroom stuff and a container to carry it back and forth.

She washed all the clothes in her room and found over a hundred pairs of socks—she chose the best thirty or forty pairs to take with her, plus underwear, maybe five or six pairs of pants and jeans, turtlenecks and T-shirts, workout clothes, pajamas, sweaters, light jacket, heavy jacket, gloves, sneakers, and boots.

She wanted some of her books with her and took maybe thirty—some reference books like a dictionary and thesaurus and some of her childhood and teenage favorites. She took a huge assortment of memory-makers, maybe fifteen framed photos and a bulletin board with more photos tacked on, and some posters, her computer, and, of course, her boombox and CDs. She talked to her three roommates in advance—one of them had a refrigerator and another was bringing a hot pot. They decided they didn't want a TV (there's no room for it anyway) and the college has its own phone system.

It sounds like more stuff than any one person could want or need, and most kids don't have a hundred pairs of socks! Still, remember that your child will be living at college, not just visiting. Scanning your lists and talking to other kids and parents will ensure that you don't leave out anything crucial as you and your kid pack.

Lists to Get You Started

✓ underwear (at least a one to two-week supply)
✓ socks (a two to three-week supply is good)
✓ jeans and casual pants/skirts
✓ T-shirts and shirts
✓ sweatshirts and sweaters
✓ shoes and boots
✓ bathrobe and flip-flops

✓ dress-up clothes if needed: sport jacket, dress pants, suits, dresses
✓ accessories: belts, scarves, ties, jewelry
✓ sports clothes and equipment
✓ jackets and coats
✓ rain gear (including umbrella)
✓ winter gear if needed: hats, gloves, mufflers, earmuffs

✓ sheets and pillowcases
✓ blankets and comforter
✓ mattress pad
✓ foam "egg-crate" mattress pad (dorm mattresses tend to have smooth, hard surfaces)
✓ bedspread, if desired
✓ towels

✓ bathroom supplies and container to carry them to bathroom
✓ first-aid supplies
✓ medications
✓ shaving gear
✓ toiletries and cosmetics

✓ laundry bag or basket
✓ detergent, stain remover, fabric softener
✓ alarm clock
✓ desk and/or bedside lamp (check college's rules before buying halogen lamps, which can be dangerous)
✓ music equipment
✓ desk supplies
✓ reference and other books
✓ bulletin board (an important organizing tool)
✓ calendar
✓ full-length mirror (some dorm rooms lack this)
✓ storage crates and accessories (over-door hooks, under-bed boxes, etc.)

✓ hangers
✓ rug
✓ wastebasket
✓ wall decorations

Other Handy Items

There are a few items that often don't get included and that many kids wish they had. Some examples:

Stamps or stamped envelopes—It's sometimes not easy to find a post office near campus, and letters can sit around for days and weeks before finally getting mailed. A supply of envelopes and stamps will encourage your kid to write to you and to others, like grandparents, who'd love to know how things are going. Stamped and addressed postcards, on which the message can be very short, are even easier for preoccupied students to make use of.

Address list or book—Many kids have never owned an address book, but it will be a big help to them now. Write in the complete addresses and phone numbers of family members, close friends, and anyone else your kid might want to write or call.

Medications, prescriptions to be refilled, prescriptions for glasses or contact lenses—Keep duplicates of these items yourself, and make sure your child knows where prescriptions should be filled for the health plan you are using.

Tool kit—This doesn't have to be large or elaborate, but a small set of tools, including screwdrivers, pliers, hammer, and heavy-duty scissors, plus tape of various kinds (masking, transparent, duct), will be used many times just in the first couple of weeks.

Eating utensils (fork, spoon, knife, mug, roll of paper towels)— Useful for late-night pizza, coffee or tea, as well as soup warmed in a hot pot.

Extension cords—These are easy to forget, and in most dorm rooms they are essential.

Hangers—Even easier to forget, and even more essential.

Laundry bag—One mother said, "A big laundry bag is crucial to your kid's survival."

Rolls of quarters for laundry machines—This sounds absurd; surely your kid can acquire these on his own. But college students unanimously agree that this is a tremendously helpful item for parents to include. It's not always easy on campus to get the number of quarters needed for a month's worth of laundry, especially when the urge to clean strikes late at night, and having them handy in the desk drawer means one less thing to think about while studying for a midterm.

Sharing the Shopping

Old cultural habits die hard, and mothers still tend to do more of the shopping and packing with their kids than fathers do. Sometimes this can make dads feel left out, especially divorced fathers.

> *Even though we have joint custody, my daughter keeps most of her stuff at her mother's house, and so that's where she did all her packing. She told me about it when I asked how the preparations were going, but it was clear that all the energy and excitement was centered around the activity at my ex-wife's, and I didn't feel involved in it at all.*

Obviously it's not practical to divide the packing between two homes, so it can be difficult for both parents to be part of the process, particularly if the painful or hostile feelings surrounding the divorce are still strong. But when parents can share these preparations in some agreed-upon way, their kids feel less stress and guilt about hurting Mom's or Dad's feelings.

Getting a Commuter Student Organized

If your child will be living at home and commuting to college, you may think there's not much you need to do, apart from helping him choose his courses and adjusting to a different schedule. But many parents discover that some planning ahead and preparing for changes makes the transition easier for everyone.

You and your child might want to consider rearranging his room to some extent. Perhaps some of the high school paraphernalia can be put away; maybe he'll need a computer if he doesn't already have one; an armchair and a TV (if there's room) might make the room more clearly his space and provide some privacy and independence.

Talking over the possibilities also provides opportunities to talk about the changes you anticipate in your lives once college classes start. For example, do you expect your kid to continue doing whatever household chores have been her responsibility in high school? Or do you feel she could contribute a bit more now that she's in college? It's a good idea to discuss these questions early and settle on a plan everyone can be happy with, so your child will have one less thing to worry about during the first confusing weeks.

Reducing the Stress

Helping your kid pack for college can turn into a power struggle if you let it; it can also produce hurt feelings as you and your child argue and reject each other's ideas. Try to remember that arguments about packing often represent a safe way to express tension that's really connected to larger and scarier issues; this realization can go a long way toward preventing you from blowing up when your kid wants to pack only his oldest and rattiest T-shirts, and keeping you calm when he says he hates the plaid sheets you just bought on sale. He probably needs a nonthreatening outlet for the nervous confusion seething inside him; let him know you understand he's worried and you know it's normal, and maybe you can even coax a laugh from the situation. And for most parents and kids, between the arguments are many moments of cheerful cooperation and reminiscence. In any case, the packing will be over soon.

It Won't All Fit in the Car!

If you plan to drive your child to college, the packing is easier in one way at least: You don't have to worry about shipping and possible breakage. Many experienced students recommend using plastic garbage bags instead of suitcases: suitcases take up lots of valuable space in a dorm room, and there's often nowhere to keep them except under the bed, an area that may be needed as a supplement to the minuscule dresser drawers. Garbage bags, on the other hand, can be tossed out or folded flat to keep for future use. Do remember, though, that your kid will need a case of some kind for vacation travel by plane, train, or bus, as well as an overnight bag for possible weekends away.

No matter how you pack, you'll probably be amazed at the amount of stuff your child is taking to college. By the time you load up the clothes, shoes, bedding, sports equipment, bathroom gear, books, desk supplies, music library and listening equipment, desk lamp (dorm lighting is notoriously awful), and some plastic storage cubes or shelves to hold all these things, there's barely room in the car for the driver. Add a computer, a TV, and a small refrigerator, and it looks hopeless. Some families end up taking two cars in order to fit in the people as well as the things.

If you foresee that cramming everything into the car will be a problem, consider renting a van, or borrowing one from a generous friend. Call well in advance for rentals—vans go fast at this time of year.

UPS to the Rescue

If you can't fit everything into the car, also consider shipping some of the stuff to the college to await your child's arrival, and planning to buy some of what's needed once you get there. Both of these options are probably necessities if your child is going to school by plane, train, or bus; plastic garbage bags won't work on these modes of transportation, and in any case, there will be far too much for your child to manage, even if the airline allowed seventeen suitcases.

If you're not going to drive your kid to college, you won't want to let the planning and packing slide until the last minute. You'll receive information from the college about how to address shipping boxes and where they can be picked up when your child arrives. Think about shipping as much stuff as possible—clothes, bedding, books, unbreakable furnishings, tapes and CDs, even audio equipment and computer parts in their original boxes and packing materials.

My son went to college by plane, so he couldn't take everything with him. We shipped his computer and two large cartons of clothes. I had ordered sheets and pillows and a quilt from a catalog and had them sent directly to the college. When he got there, he bought other stuff locally—a laundry basket, stackable storage cubes, and a lamp.

An advantage of cardboard shipping boxes is that they can be broken down and stored flat under a bed for re-use. When you pack them, either for shipping or to take in the car, keep in mind that you or your kid will probably have to carry them up the dormitory stairs; they should be light enough for one person to pick up without a forklift.

As you wade through the items to be packed, remember that this isn't the last time you'll be in touch with your child until next May. Perhaps you can plan to bring the winter clothing on Parents' Weekend, for example. Items that won't be needed immediately can also be shipped later—they'll get there soon enough.

Deciding How to Travel

How your kid will get to college depends on many variables, including time and distance; but if at all possible, include him in the discussion and let him express his preference on the subject. Some kids prefer to get the emotional farewells over with at home; they may be afraid that a tearful scene as their parents leave the campus and drive away will be more than they can handle. For such kids, traveling by bus, train, or plane can provide a buffer zone between the security of home and the uncertainty of college. Other kids feel that their parents' presence will be something to hold on to in a strange new world, and they prefer to arrive by car. And driving appeals to many parents for their own reasons.

> I took my son to school the first year, and I was glad I did. Seeing the campus helped me a lot. I always make a mental image anyway, and it's nice to have it be close to reality. Meeting his roommate helped, too. I liked him and felt he'd be someone my son could depend on.

Whatever you decide about transportation to college, you can feel certain that plenty of your child's classmates will be arriving in the same way, and with the same hopes and fears.

CHAPTER FIVE

Out of the House and into the Dorm

You've made a plan and a schedule for your child's departure, and the day is drawing near alarmingly fast. Are you wondering whether to have a farewell dinner before your kid leaves? Opinions vary on this question. On the one hand, it marks the occasion as important and meaningful to everyone; on the other, it may well turn into an awkward, silent gathering because everyone is treating it as a formal ceremony but no one can come up with anything sufficiently profound to say.

It's probably best to take your cue from your child's feelings about it. Try not to feel hurt if the idea is turned down and your kid spends the entire last day and evening, and most of the night, with friends or alone in her room with the music blasting at top volume. A farewell dinner may be more acceptable to your child if you join forces with another family whose kid is about to leave for college; a casual gathering—maybe a barbecue or picnic—for a group a little larger than your immediate family can provide both a sense of occasion and an animated sociability that takes the spotlight off your kid.

In fact, if you've been looking forward to any kind of last-chance, in-depth, heart-to-heart talk with your child, don't count on it happening. In some families it works out perfectly, with a conversation that's satisfying to all concerned, but for many it's an ordeal that dribbles awkwardly into clichés and stock phrases.

Driving Your Kid to College

And now you're off! Driving your kid to college for the first time can be one of the hardest things you've ever done. The realization that your child is actually leaving home hits you, and you feel both incredibly worried and totally bereft.

For your kid, however, it's quite different: He's simultaneously leaving home and arriving somewhere new and unknown. In the car many kids are silent and preoccupied. They're scared, but they don't want to admit it to themselves or to their parents; they're uncertain of what to expect and how they'll cope, but they're unwilling to reveal this uncertainty. At the same time they're unable to think about anything else, so they say almost nothing. Feeling this way is normal and extremely common: A student who read this book in manuscript underlined the previous two sentences and wrote "Yes!" in the margin.

The drive itself sometimes feels suspended in time and space between two worlds, and the journey plays out in various ways for different families.

We all drove up the day before and stayed overnight with friends near the college. That was good because it kind of eased us into it, but our daughter was very nervous. We took two cars—we couldn't fit everything into one—and that worked out really well: First our daughter drove three hours with her younger sister, then with me, and then with my husband, so we each had our time alone with her to say good-bye.

Especially if this is the oldest child, many families make the journey as a group, and they wouldn't consider doing it any other way. For them and their kids, it feels right.

Our younger kids came with us when we took our oldest son to college. It was good for them; they could see where he was going to be living, and it helped them feel he wasn't gone forever. But our second son went by plane, so the younger ones couldn't go along, and they were quite upset.

Other parents see the question differently, though.

We made the choice not to take our younger two along. My friend took her whole family; she wanted them there to make it a kind of commemorative moment of "This is our eldest going off to college." But I thought it would be very distracting and even more nervewracking for our daughter. And I didn't want to have to think about anyone's needs except hers; I wanted to focus on her.

Your decision about this will reflect your knowledge of your own family and of your kid, who may well have strong feelings about it one way or the other. There's no one right way to do this, so don't worry overmuch about how other people handle the question—just do what feels right for your family.

Experienced parents emphasize that the journey is the time to say good-bye, to reiterate those last important pieces of advice, and to express again your love for and confidence in your kid. It's often impossible to find time and space to do this after you reach the campus, and you'll feel bad if you leave with important things still unsaid. In addition, some kids do want to talk about what's happening.

We talked a lot on the drive up about all kinds of things. It was a strange feeling to have him going out of my life like that—I started missing him before I dropped him off. We talked about that, about what it was like when I went to college and what he thought it was going to be like for him, about how it's not easy to start someplace new.

But sometimes it's difficult for parents to express what they're feeling.

> My daughter was always home, she never went to camp or anything. It really wasn't until we were on our way to the college, two hundred miles or so, that I realized how far away she would be and that I would be leaving her and coming back without her. That was so hard. The whole way I was trying not to cry because I didn't want her to feel bad. I was worried, and sad, and already very lonely.

Parents as well as their kids may be nervous and scared, and also unwilling to admit these feelings. One father said:

> It's an easy drive to the college, but somehow there was a rush to leave the house, so I decided to stop on the way and get coffee. Then, about forty-five minutes later, I stopped again to get something to eat. But it made my son crazy to keep stopping all the time. What I saw as a leisurely trip because we had so much time, he saw as intolerable delays. Finally he said, "Can we not stop any more until we get there?"

Most parents don't employ such delaying tactics on purpose. But stretching the journey in this way can be a means of holding on to a child for just a few more hours and postponing the moment of letting go.

Sending Your Child to College Alone

Sending a kid off alone on a plane or train is difficult in a different way.

> It was too far to drive her to school, so we put her on a plane. It was hard for her; she had to lug her suitcases and make lots of changes and connections. I felt bad about not taking her, it must have been awful for her to arrive alone by plane.

Luckily they have this system where students volunteer to go to the airport and meet kids who come from far away; they take them to the campus to find their room and everything. But still, I felt bad.

A welcoming system such as this college has is a great idea, although it may not be feasible in large cities whose airports have multiple terminals. Still, it's worth checking on the college's arrangements for kids who are traveling alone; if there are none, perhaps you can find a friend or a friend's friend who'd be willing to meet your kid's plane and escort her to the college.

If You're Divorced

Taking or sending a kid to college is more complicated when parents are divorced. Each set of parents has to find a way that works for them and for their child. One father saw it in a traditional light:

My ex-wife will take our daughter to college. It wouldn't be good for both of us to go, and it's natural for a mother to help a daughter set up her room.

Another set of parents worked things out together.

All of us went to the airport—me, my ex, and our younger child—and helped our son; he had a million suitcases. We've both stayed very involved with both kids' lives, and we both wanted to say good-bye to him.

Sometimes it's hard to come to a compromise.

When my former wife said she wanted to be the one to take our daughter to school, my reaction was, "I want to come, too." She said okay, but after a while I realized that it would be an easier experience for our daughter if I didn't go. So I said, "Fine, but I'll take our son to college when he goes in two years."

Especially for noncustodial parents, it can be very important to be there to say good-bye to a child.

My second wife didn't come to see my son off, though they're very close. But there was a real sweetness, a beauty about having what had been our nuclear family there as a unit (even if it was just a temporary illusion) at the moment of his departure.

But for a kid, having both parents present may be an added strain at what's already a tension-filled time. One student said:

It was good going to college with just my mom; it was the way I wanted it. I didn't want to elongate the good-bye thing, and I didn't want to have divorced-parent problems while I was leaving for school, because I was thinking about enough as it was. I asked my dad not to come. He wanted to come with my mom, because he was afraid she'd get hysterical and be unable to drive after she left me there, but I said no, she'll be okay, and besides, you won't fit in the car.

Finally There! Chaos, Anxiety, and Excitement

You've followed the directions you received, and now you're lining up with the hundreds of other parents and kids in cars, vans, even trucks who are jockeying for position. Whether you turn in through a beautiful brick archway or steer your way between monolithic dormitory blocks, the process of arriving at school is awkward and fraught with anxiety. Knowing that all the other families are in the same boat can provide a measure of comfort.

> *We stayed in a motel near the college the night before, and we saw another girl, obviously a freshman, and her family in the restaurant. The next morning I went to take my shower and I could hear their voices echoing through the pipes and the walls. The girl was wailing, "I don't want to stay here, don't make me stay," and the parents were saying, "No, no, you have to stay," and all I could think was, Thank God it's not my child. It was so mournful and terrible, and I thought how awful it would be to have to force your kid out of the car and drive away. It was everything you didn't want to hear your child saying and feeling, coming through the pipes of the motel.*

An experience like that can make you feel (selfishly and guiltily) great—your kid is in much better shape than others, or than you'd feared. But what if it's your child who's wailing? First, it probably won't be; most kids aren't nearly this extreme and open about their fears and self-doubts. But if it is, try to stay cool and wait it out. Be sympathetic but firm: You understand your child feels completely panicked, but she's here and she'll have to stick it out, at least for a while. Set a date for a further discussion of the options, perhaps planning a second visit to the campus so you can talk things over face-to-face. Remind her that everyone else is scared, too, even if they hide their feelings more than she does. Tell her you'll be available by phone, e-mail, or whatever, whenever she needs to communicate with you; this kind of emotional situation is not the time to worry about extra-high phone bills.

Don't say you're sure your child will get over it in a couple of days—that sounds as if you're making light of feelings that to her are terrifyingly real and overwhelming. But be sure to let her know you have confidence in her ability to manage life at college, even if she doesn't love it.

Of course, you hope she will come to love it very soon, but by not saying that, you avoid setting up an I-told-you-so in the future.

The actual move-in day for freshmen is often chaotic and confusing, though the intensity of the turmoil varies from one college to another. One parent described the ideal arrival:

> Our daughter's college had a streamlined, very welcoming, unbelievably organized opening day. We were kind of on automatic pilot because we were so nervous, but they took care of everything. They had hundreds of upperclassmen there showing you where to park, telling you what line to stand in and where to get the room key, lifting the luggage, moving her in—all of it. It relieved a tremendous amount of anxiety, which was wonderful, because when you feel stressed about everything, it rubs off on your kid. It was a flawless opening day.

Everyone should be so lucky! Here is a more typical description:

> It's a nightmare—unloading the stuff, you can't get near the dorm, and all the other thirteen hundred people are trying to park in the same three locations. It's really horrible. We got there early and they didn't start checking kids in until nine o'clock, but we could pull up to the dorm and unload and then move so other families could do the same thing. So here were all these distraught families with their freshmen, with everything piled up around the door and the bedding on top of the piles, it looked like The Grapes of Wrath. Then our son went to check in while we started carrying stuff upstairs; the boxes were too big and too heavy so it was exhausting, and it took forever until he finally got back with the key. That no parent had a heart attack was amazing, because it was late August, incredibly hot and humid, and there were all these overweight parents carrying things up four flights of stairs.

In retrospect it will be funny, but at the time it can make you crazy, even though you know that tension is stretching your patience thinner than usual and things probably aren't quite as awful as they seem.

It's possible that your kid already has some experience of the college. Some sports teams arrive early for a week or so of practice before classes start, and a freshman team member will have learned a fair amount about the campus and how it works by the time official freshman orientation begins. She may not have moved into her own room, however; some colleges open only one dorm for the teams, so that she'll have to move into her own room now along with everyone else.

If you participated in a parent orientation program at the college earlier in the summer, you probably feel a comforting degree of familiarity with the campus. But the actual arrival day is still pretty overwhelming.

Many parents who've been through taking a kid to college advise arriving as early as possible. You avoid some of the crush and confusion in parking lots and dorm hallways, and you won't feel so rushed if you have to shop for last-minute necessities or pick up shipped packages that are waiting in a storage room somewhere. Many parents also like arriving early so their kid can have first pick of the beds and closets.

We got to the room first and helped him decide which side was better. We opened all the dresser drawers and switched one that was broken. We also switched the mattresses so he had the less lumpy one—not very nice of us, I guess. His roommate wasn't happy when he arrived, although now they're good friends.

Another parent said:

Our daughter definitely wanted to be the first in the room. She remembered that her older sister's roommate was already

*there when we arrived for her first year, and she learned from
that experience. That's why we left the night before.*

This strategy doesn't always work out as planned—kids
and parents may feel uncomfortable about taking advantage
in this way and may also worry that it will get the roommate
relationship off to a bad start. Some colleges take steps to
prevent this from happening.

*We arrived first, but the college had a strict policy that no
decision about beds could be made before all the roommates
were there. So we followed the rules and put all our daughter's
stuff in the common room. In fact, no one got to unpack until
after the dorm meeting that night when they talked about fair
ways to choose, maybe trading in midyear, and so on. It was
the opposite of the camp experience where you rushed up early
to get your kid the best bed.*

However, this kind of systematic approach is the exception
rather than the rule.

If your child is first in the room, you're all standing there
wondering how this mountain of stuff is possibly going to
fit in this tiny room, even without another person's things,
when the roommate arrives. If you're not there first, you
walk in carrying a gigantic box or dragging a heavy suitcase,
and a group of strangers gives you a suspicious look. You
and your kid both wonder, Is this the right room?

It doesn't help that the room itself may not be what
you've envisioned. Many dorm rooms are small, grimy,
poorly lit, and badly furnished. One mother said, "I was
appalled by the furniture, all chipped and scratched with
dust bunnies in all the drawers—it was disgusting. And the
walls looked like cinderblock painted a kind of dead gray
color. I thought it was incredibly depressing." Another recalled, "I thought the room could have been cleaner, but
my husband said, 'It won't stay that way, so what's the
difference?' "

The initial encounter between roommates and whatever family members accompany them is inevitably awkward. Kids and parents alike are covertly sizing up the others, crossing their fingers as they try to predict whether this relationship will work out. Parents' protective feelings tend to emerge full force; you may want to rearrange the furniture to give your child the most space, light, air, or whatever, or you may notice with resentment that the roommate has far more stuff than your kid has and he's encroaching on your kid's desktop or wall space.

There was no room for anything. I helped my son put stuff in the minute closet and figure out where the storage crates could go. I tried to suggest a way of arranging things, but the roommate's parents got quite upset, so finally I said, The boys will have to do it, this is ridiculous.

To add to the general awkwardness, as soon as the roommates arrive, your child may start pretending you're not there. It's hard not to be annoyed when your kid acts as if you're an embarrassment, but try not to express your irritation. Keep in mind that your kid is facing a sea of diverse strangers with whom she has to establish some sort of contact; she's also going to share a room with a person she probably didn't choose and knows nothing about. And you won't be there to help, so she's likely to feel she has to start this relationship off on her own, without relying on your input.

My daughter is in a triple (converted from a double), and there was some discussion around closet and cabinet space because it really wasn't adequate. One girl had gotten there several days early for tennis team practice and had taken the best storage space. My daughter and the third girl weren't happy, but she told me that after the parents left, they talked about it and the first girl moved some of her stuff. Everything was fine after that.

Remember, too, that sometimes parents really do behave in ways that are embarrassing to their children.

When we got to our son's room, his roommate was already there with his parents. Both beds were on the floor, not stacked up as bunks, and it seemed as if between the two boys, there was way too much stuff. The roommate's parents started giving advice on how to arrange everything, and the father was being very directive, almost bossy, which made everyone uncomfortable. We felt, It's our son's room, not ours, he has to make the decisions. Finally all the parents went out to a parents' orientation program. When we got back the boys had stacked the beds and arranged all the furniture. They were proud of themselves; they'd worked it out together—it was a good way to start. Your instinct is to help as much as possible, but it's better to pull back and keep your hands off.

This is difficult advice to follow, and you have to try to gauge your own kid's wishes and needs. Lots of moms find it impossible to leave without making their child's bed, and many kids welcome this bit of help. Some definitely need to "nest in" themselves; others are happy to have parents hang around and help put things away and find a place to stack the storage crates, and this activity helps parents, too. Just stay alert for signals that your child needs time alone or with the roommate to begin making the room his own, and remember that rearranging the furniture together is a good way for roommates to get acquainted.

Parents tend to do what they need, not necessarily what kids need. You have to try to be in tune with what your kid wants on that day. It can be tricky. At first it seemed my daughter wanted me not to help, then she wanted me to. She kept saying, "I don't know where to start." Finally I told her, "We can unpack now or you can do it after we leave," and she said, "Oh, let's do it." So we did, and I think she was very relieved. Afterwards she said, "Now the room looks like it's mine." She had sounded like she didn't want help, couldn't ask for it, almost pushed it away, but she really did want it.

If you have time to hang around but don't want to get in your kid's way, take off for an hour or so and scout the nearby stores for essential missing items: Frequently mentioned examples are duct tape, more hangers and extension cords, a lamp, a mirror, a bedside table or crate, even a bookshelf (many dorms don't supply them).

My impression was that my son and his roommate were glad to have help, especially running errands in the car. I know people who went up for orientation in August and saw their kid's room and took measurements, but we had no idea what would be needed until we got there, so we had to buy several things.

This is a great way to take your mind off your worries about your child and to feel you're doing something obviously useful before saying good-bye.

But try to remember that this is an extremely tense and difficult time for all the entering freshmen. What your kid says and does on this first day may bear little relationship to his real feelings about anything—including you, himself, his new roommate, and the whole prospect of beginning college. A mother recalled:

I took my son to college, and when I saw his room, I was upset—it was so cold and impersonal, and the windows were totally bare. His roommate wasn't there yet, and as we unpacked I asked my son if he wanted me to go out and get some curtains. He gave me that don't-be-so-stupid look and said, "Oh, Mom, get real—who needs curtains?"

I left soon after that and went to spend a week with an old friend who lives near the college. On my way home I stopped to see how my son was doing. I told him the room looked pretty good, and he replied, "Yeah, but it's kind of bare-looking. Do you have time to get some curtains and put them up?"

Throughout the day, the level of tension is likely to remain high. Your child is jumping, or being pushed, into an alien environment full of strangers. You want to protect and help your kid, but you also know you'll have to leave him to manage on his own. All of you are clinging together one minute and pushing away the next. Many parents describe walking across campus with their kid, except that he's not really with them, he's several paces ahead or behind, already moving away from them. Yet when you reach the cafeteria or wherever, he makes it clear he wants to sit with you. It can be difficult to keep up with these changing signals, and despite everyone's wish for a harmonious day full of good family feelings, you may find yourselves snapping at one another for no reason. Reminding yourself of the anxiety that burdens your kid can help stifle those impatient comments that you'll regret later.

At some point during the hectic activity, take a moment to look over the schedule of events for the day. You may decide you don't want to get involved in any of them; many parents prefer to take their kid to lunch and perhaps walk around the campus with a map, figuring out where the library and bookstore and other important buildings are.

Various things were planned for kids and for parents, but we ignored them. Lots of parents were walking around with name tags on and so on, but we tend not to do that. And our son didn't want to do the formal stuff, and didn't want us to do it either, so we did nothing that was planned for us. We took him out to dinner, then he walked to the car with us and we said good-bye. It was perfect.

But other parents want to participate. It's a way to get to know a little about the campus and also to reassure yourself again that other parents and other kids feel just as much at sea as you do.

> *Our daughter and her roommate were instant soulmates, and we liked her parents a lot. All of us had lunch together and then went back to the girls' room. It was pretty well organized by that time, and I got a feeling that the two of them were hiding out in their room, clinging to the one person they could trust, and a little afraid to venture any farther—and maybe we were, too. Finally the other mom and I said we all had to go to the opening convocation for new students. Both girls were reluctant, but when we got there they sat with some other freshmen and we sat with the other parents. Sitting out on that beautiful lawn with the trees overhead was a nice way to wrap up a hectic day, and I was glad there were some activities to help them get into the swing of things.*

Another parent recalled feeling incompetent and adrift in strange surroundings; being told what to do when was helpful.

> *In the morning there was a meeting for the parents, with questions and answers; meanwhile the kids were getting their photos taken for student ID cards, I think. Then there was lunch in the cafeteria, which was kind of tense; our son didn't know anyone, but he didn't want to be sitting with his parents in this big dining hall and he decided he didn't like the food— he was obviously nervous and uncomfortable. Then the dean and the president addressed the kids on the lawn while the parents stood at the back. It was clear that parents weren't welcome to stay after that; our son knew it and we did, too, so we left.*

Do what feels right for you and your child. You may decide to attend all the events, or none of them, or pick and choose what sounds interesting. However, if there are required activities for your child, do make sure he gets to

them on time and that he's not out at the discount store
with you at that moment. Don't be surprised if your kid
seems distracted or spaced out; he's got a lot on his mind
right now. One third-year student probably spoke for many
when he said, "We went out to lunch and then listened to
speeches on the first day? I don't remember any of it."

Saying Good-bye

Actually saying good-bye and leaving is hard, sometimes in
surprising ways. It has to be done, though, and it's best not
to hang around too long.

> *Once our son's room was set up, it was tempting to stay on
> longer, and I would have liked to. But I knew he needed to be
> on his own and start to adjust to being there.*

Many colleges let parents know when their stay should
end; one printed schedule for freshman arrival day said,
"4:00 P.M.: Parents depart," making things perfectly clear.
But it's also likely that your kid will convey that it's time.

> *Our daughter said good-bye sooner than we were ready. You
> just wait for that moment when you see that it's natural for
> you to leave, it's clear they don't need you anymore, so you
> exit, hard as that may be. When our daughter was ready for
> us to leave, it was as if she said, Okay, good-bye, I've got
> things to do. I said to my husband, "She's dismissed us, she's
> ready to get on with the college scene."*

This kind of clear signal from the kid is very common.
Another parent remembered:

> *She didn't want us to go, she walked around campus with her
> dad because he hadn't seen it before, we went out to eat, then
> to a reception at the president's house, then back to her room.*

At that point she said, "It's okay for you to go." You can tell when it's time, and there's no sense lingering, she had to start getting to know the other kids.

And still another recalled:

On the second night there was a barbecue for parents and kids, but some parents had already left. We asked our son if he wanted us to stay or go, and he said, Just go. We let him choose. We had clearly finished everything we needed to do. I would have been happy to stay longer, but I could see it was time to go.

Parents are sometimes disappointed that their farewell moment isn't a big, dramatic event; it may feel anticlimactic. For others, the drama may be intense. Whichever way your family plays this scene, it's not easy.

When it was time for us to leave, we were in tears, she was in tears, she seemed scared, and we were scared to be leaving our daughter at this huge, impersonal place, wondering what would happen to her among so many different kinds of people. On the way home we stopped two or three times and left messages on her answering machine—we didn't think we'd get that emotional, but we did.

And even if you promise you won't let your feelings get out of control, watching your child make the first tentative steps into a new world can be heartwrenching.

At the end of the afternoon there was a reception in the big courtyard in the middle of campus; the parents stood in line to meet the president of the college, the kids stood in another line to sign the registration book. I could see my son in the line (he's tall), and he was all alone. My husband told me not to go over to him, but I did, and he said, "I'm all right; I just don't have any friends." It was awful, but he didn't want me with him so I went back. Afterwards we went back to the dorm and it was time to say good-bye. I was last; I hugged him, and he gave me this petrified smile that said, I'm gonna make it, and that was it.

Another mother said:

Our daughter came down to see us off and we took pictures in front of her dorm. I saw tears in her eyes, but she was holding it; she was standing with her roommate and another girl, so I didn't feel I was leaving her all by herself. Then I gave her a hug, and we walked away. I turned around and she waved good-bye, and I didn't start crying until we got to the car where she wouldn't see me. I was in tears all the way home.

A common theme in parents' descriptions of their good-byes is that it goes by much too fast, and they don't have a chance to say all the important things they'd planned. There may be too many other people standing around, so you feel uncomfortable talking about such personal and emotional issues. Or you may have slightly outstayed your welcome and you can tell that your child really wants you to leave *now*. Or it may be clear that if you get emotional, your kid will break down, and that's the last thing either of you want at this moment.

This is why it's a good idea to say those things and have those conversations in the car on the way to the college or before your kid goes to the airport. Another way of handling it is to write a note and leave it in your kid's desk drawer or under her pillow where she's sure to find it that night. Some well-organized parents write a letter several days in advance and mail it so it will arrive on the morning of the child's second day at college.

However you do it, try to find a way to communicate to your kid that you love him, you're proud of him, you have confidence in his ability to succeed at college, and that you'll be available whenever he wants to ask your advice, talk over a problem, or just chat. Kids, even those whose discomfort with this kind of talk is evident, need to hear these things as they begin their college careers.

CHAPTER SIX

Adjusting to an Emptier Nest

Riding the Emotional Roller Coaster

As you drive away from the campus or leave the airport or bus station, you may feel anything from relief to intense sadness to a kind of frozen numbness. All of these reactions are normal! And you may find yourself swinging from one emotional state to another without much warning. One mother remembered:

> I cried a lot—I'm crying now talking about it. I cried most of the way home. But my husband was upbeat and excited for her. In fact, I think our emotions weren't so different; I don't feel only sadness, it's a combination of sadness and joy. I've been on an emotional roller coaster, both missing her and very happy for her.

Another said:

> When I got back from the airport, I went into her empty room and a feeling of sadness overcame me. That was the last time she'd ever live here full-time.

It isn't only women who may feel overwhelmed. A father said:

I got a speeding ticket on the way home—going probably eighty miles an hour in a forty mile-per-hour zone. I told the cop I had just dropped off my son at college—I was absolutely unable to think about anything but him.

Another father recalled:

It was the longest ride home—I had an empty, very lonely feeling, knowing I wouldn't see my daughter for a couple of months. It hit me a lot harder than I expected.

And many parents say that it's not any easier the second time around.

When our first child left for college, there was a tremendous feeling of loss and separation. I didn't expect the second to be pain-free, but I thought the prior experience would make it more routine, less painful—it didn't.

Another mother said:

My oldest child's leaving was pretty easy for me, but I think it's going to be different with my second child. I'm going to miss her tremendously. It's so idiosyncratic, the child and the situation, how you feel about that particular one leaving at that particular time.

This theme is echoed by other parents:

I was very sad when our second child left, much more than with the first. When the older one left, I still had one at home. But this was a real rite of passage for me—now the house is empty of children. I wasn't prepared for how hard this separation would be for me; it catches you off guard.

Other parents have a more muted reaction. A father recalled:

There was a sense of relief when she left. She'd been home all summer, she didn't know what to do with herself—she was ready.

For some single parents, the experience feels a bit different.

My wife and I split up about five years before our son went to college, and for me that was the biggest adjustment. The separation anxiety and all the pain had come when I left the house. By the time he went away, I was already used to not seeing him so often.

Parents sometimes feel a bit guilty that their emotions aren't more extreme. One mother explained:

Going home, I felt relieved and reassured—very different from other parents I've talked to. I had been so worried about things like how would the roommate situation work out, but it all seemed fine. Also we met a lot of people who made me feel good—the freshman counselor, the resident assistant in the dorm, the dean; everybody seemed eager to make the kids feel settled in and comfortable. So I wasn't sad on the way home; I just felt, Oh, this will be good for my kid. I hadn't expected to feel relieved; I'd expected to be very upset. It was only later, after I got home and got back into my life and realized that he wasn't here, that I really missed him.

Whenever it hits them, parents are often surprised, and sometimes upset, at the intensity of their feelings. After all, they've been preparing for their child's departure for months—why can't they take it in stride? But, though you know that going to college is what your child needs to do now, and you wouldn't want to deny him this opportunity to learn and develop and move toward adulthood, the reality of it can be very painful. For one thing, you miss your child's physical presence in the house and the sound of his voice. Even if there are other children at home, you may feel lonely for the one who's left the nest.

The sense of loss may be even more powerful for single parents.

My daughter had spent summers away, but that didn't help— I was desolated. After she left, the house was empty; there was no trail of shoes and clothing through the rooms, no doors slamming to let me know she was home. There was quiet that was not welcome. A kid livens things up; she had her friends, her music, she brought a different perspective into the house. When it's only the two of you, there's a big hole when the child leaves—a big hole. You miss stuff like the phone ringing, but really you miss your kid.

Sometimes your child's step away from you and into an unknown environment feels like a rejection. Mixed with your sadness and your fears and concerns, there may be a little anger, unreasonable though you know it is; this major change in your lives is scary for you as well as for your kid. It's a signal that time is passing, that you're getting older (old enough to have a child in college)—and it's a signal that's pretty hard to ignore.

Strategies for Getting Through It

The image of a hole—in the family, in the home, in one's sense of emotional completeness—is used by a striking number of parents. Most of them find ways to begin filling this hole, often right away.

We didn't go straight home after we dropped off our daughter. A friend had told us it was very hard to come home immediately to an empty house, so we went to the beach and spent two days walking by the shore and prowling in flea markets.

*We were so grateful for the advice; for us it was the best way
to start sorting out our feelings.*

Another parent said:

*We took our son to college on Friday and had planned to stay
until Sunday, but on Saturday we decided it was better to
make the break. We went to stay with a friend on the way
home—it was a nice distraction from the heavy emotions we'd
been experiencing.*

As soon as you do get home, write your child a letter
or send a card with a note. Taking a definite action that
affirms your connection with your child will make you feel
better. And even in this era of electronic communications,
kids love to get actual mail. There's something comforting
about a physical object waiting in the mailbox; it's a reassurance that they haven't been forgotten.

If your child's college is not too far away, you can derive
comfort from the thought that it will be easy to see her.

*One thing I feel about her being away, I can imagine her
coming back fairly often—for the high school homecoming
game, for instance, and for the Jewish holidays. It's easy because it's close; I think she won't be gone for a long, uninter-
rupted period of time because it'll be so convenient to come
home. I wouldn't feel so cheerful if we lived far away.*

Strange as it sounds, it also helps to get started right
away on making any future travel arrangements that you'll
need. Planes and trains are generally sold out far in advance
for the Thanksgiving and Christmas vacations; making reser-
vations now for your child is positive evidence that you will
see her soon. If you plan to go to Parents' Weekend at your
child's college, reserve your hotel room now; especially in
small towns, they fill up early. Also consider making a dinner reservation for that weekend; almost every first-year stu-

dent wants to go out with parents for some noninstitutional food, and you may not have many choices if you wait till you get there.

Getting together with friends whose children have also just left for college is perhaps the best way to get through this initial period. You can compare notes on how your kids, and you, are doing and trade tips on what helps and what doesn't.

> *I talked to my friends about everything my son was going through, like roommate problems and deciding to drop a class. It's just like when they were teething or being toilet-trained— you get better information from your friends than from any other source.*

Naturally this works only with people you can trust to be understanding and sympathetic, but if you're fortunate enough to have the makings of such a support group available, by all means take advantage of it. Talking about your own feelings and your concerns for your child can provide valuable perspective. You may come away feeling relieved that your kid isn't having as many problems as some others are and is handling things better than you'd realized. Even if the going is rough for your kid right now, and you feel envious of other parents whose children seem to be having a wonderful time, their concern will make you feel better and can provide reassurance that things are likely to improve soon.

If the children of this group are friends, you may even learn what your child is telling her friends about her adjustment to college. It may be different from what you've heard from her. Some kids call home only when they're unhappy, giving parents a warped view of the overall picture; learning that your child's friends have heard she's having a great time can be a big relief.

Other kids take the opposite approach and edit out all the problems when they call home; perhaps they don't want to worry their parents or perhaps they need to prove to themselves that they can cope without Mom or Dad's help. It's important to respect this desire, but if you discover through your kid's friends' parents that things aren't as rosy as you've been led to believe, you may decide to make an extra phone call just to reiterate, in general terms, your love and support.

It helps to remind yourself that college, especially at first, isn't all wonderful. Parents often develop unrealistic expectations, partly because they hope so fervently that these will be the best years of their kids' lives and partly because they tend to suppress the painful memories of their own college years and remember only the good parts. It's important to acknowledge that college, like the rest of life, is never perfect and that every kid experiences some difficulties. Trying to keep your expectations in tune with reality will help you respond sympathetically to your child's inevitable problems.

Changes in Daily Life

As the sharp sense of loneliness and emptiness begins to fade, parents find that their lives settle into a new kind of normalcy.

> As we waved good-bye, my heart was breaking; my child was leaving and it was awful. But the reality is, it's not so bad. I feel a big hole and I miss him terribly, but seven weeks later I feel more comfortable that he's there: I don't cry anymore.

Of course, the differences are still very noticeable: The phone doesn't ring nearly as often; the piles of laundry, sneakers, and papers that littered the house are drastically reduced; there's one less person to help with the dishes; and it's much too quiet. You may notice that family pets are strongly affected by a child's departure; dogs especially often seem depressed and may cling for a while to family members who are still at home, following them from room to room to make sure they won't disappear, too.

Our dog took to sleeping next to our son's bed every night—it was almost as if she believed that would make him return. I understood how she felt—I found myself setting a place for him for dinner and waiting to hear him come in the door.

Younger siblings certainly are affected by an older brother or sister's leaving for college. When the oldest of two departs, the younger becomes in some ways an only child. Many parents see their younger child first missing the older one intensely and then beginning to enjoy being the single focus of parental attention. A younger sister said:

When my brother left, I cried a lot—my whole life was going to change, and he was never going to be home all the time again. But I got used to it. I had sports and stuff every day after school, and now I don't really mind. My parents and I have become closer—there's only three of us at dinner, and conversation is more centered on me.

And a mother said:

Our younger son misses his brother; he feels a real loss. But at the same time he enjoys the throne now and not having any distraction of attention away from him.

But some younger siblings find the change very difficult.

Our two girls are very close. When the older one left, the younger one felt she'd lost her best friend. She became very reserved, maybe as a way of defending herself; she didn't get involved in what her sister was experiencing, didn't even want to talk to her on the phone. It was too hard, and that's how she had to handle it. But the older one's leaving forced the younger one to talk to us instead of to her sister, and it helped us get closer to her.

Many younger siblings seem to blossom socially as well as within the family. Some of their increased social activity would happen anyway, simply because they're getting older, but some seems to result from being left on their own with only parents to talk to at home. And parents often relax the rules somewhat for the younger kids.

When our older daughter left for college, the younger one missed her for a while, but then she became much more involved with friends. We allowed her to do more things with her friends because her sister wasn't home to be company for her. We let her stay out later; I guess the older one breaks the parents in, and the younger one reaps the benefits. I think we mellowed a little.

Even when siblings haven't been one another's best friends, the changes take some getting used to. A younger brother said:

Before he left, I was thinking, I can't wait for this jerk to get out of the house and give me some space; I'll be able to have my friends over without him being around. But I'd rather have him home; I don't like being alone without someone to talk to on my level. I miss the closeness; now it's like a long-distance relationship. All the little stuff that's better without him doesn't add up to the more important things that aren't.

In larger families, the next-oldest child often steps into a new role.

Our oldest child's leaving was a good thing for our next child. She's now the oldest, it's given her more responsibility and more freedom, she's less in the shadow of her sister. It's had a positive effect on her.

And the kids who are still at home may forge closer ties with one another than they've had earlier.

If anything, our oldest child going off to college has done miraculous things to the relationship between the younger two—they're really good friends now; it was fantastic for them.

Parents sometimes worry about the effect of family changes on their children. A divorced mother said:

With the older two away at school, my youngest feels it's her turn to take care of me. She doesn't say so exactly, but she obviously feels the responsibility has been thrown onto her. She's become tuned in to taking care of me; she pays attention to when I'm alone and things like that.

These changes in the family dynamics aren't necessarily permanent, and the earlier patterns may reappear and read-justments occur when the college student comes home for vacation. But parents who have been preoccupied for months with the whole process of college application, ad-mission, preparation, and departure sometimes feel their younger kids have been a bit shortchanged; they welcome the chance to let a new star begin to shine, even as they know it will be just as hard to see this one leave when the time comes.

Don't be too surprised, though, if your college student resents any changes at home. Homesick kids want home to be just the way they remember it, and often they're not pleased to hear that a younger sibling appears to be taking over their place, whether it's on a team, in a classroom, or at home. It may be better to downplay the positive changes in the family, at least at first, so your kid doesn't get the impression that everyone's glad to have her gone. After a little more time has passed, the new roles will be easier for all of you to accept and even enjoy.

When the last, or the only, child leaves for college, parents sometimes breathe a sigh of relief. Friends who have already gone through this stage may tell you you're going to love having an empty nest—you'll feel so free, you'll have time to do things you've been putting off, you'll be able to get to know each other again. And to some extent they're right. Without kids at home, many couples do rediscover the pleasure they take in each other's company. Indulging in what feels like a brief return to the early days of marriage, before the kids, they rekindle the original romance, going out more often and staying out later. Single parents often find relationships deepening with friends and relatives. Single or coupled, many newly free parents throw themselves into new challenges at work or long-forgotten interests they now have time to pursue.

But it's not always easy. A single mother with a demanding job eloquently described how she coped:

> *After my son went to college, I tried to meet new people. Social life for a single person isn't built in; it takes work. I traveled a lot—maybe too much, because travel interrupts your social life, and it's sometimes hard to pick it up again when you get home. I needed to talk to people; I'd pick up the phone because I wanted to make contact. Even though I was working, there were a lot of hours to fill. I consciously expanded my life, I joined organizations to meet people. My ex-husband doesn't understand it. My son never lived with him, so he can't grasp what it's like to have your child leave.*

Another mother found ways to develop new emotional attachments.

> *I spent a lot of time with two young children who were relatives of a friend. I felt a need to reach out; I had loving to spare. You're used to hugging your kid all the time—I missed that.*

Lots of couples also find the adjustment difficult. They're used to a daily life that's focused on the children's plans and needs, and it's disorienting to have that organizing principle removed. Problems in the marriage that were covered up by preoccupation with the kids' doings may now be harder to ignore; without children around to act as buffers, parents may find themselves quarreling or growing estranged. The unresolved sense of loss created by the child's absence, emphasized by the empty time that used to be filled up with child-centered activity, makes it harder to deal with problems. Just when parents feel they need support and emotional sustenance, they may find themselves snapping impatiently at each other and entrenching themselves more firmly in antagonistic positions.

Sometimes the difficulties center around conflicting attitudes and needs. One parent may take pleasure in seeing the child begin to take on an adult's responsibilities, while the other may be unable to give up parental control and may try to keep the child in a dependent role. And some may respond to one another's attitudes in less than useful ways. For example, a protective parent may become overprotective in response to the parent who encourages the child's independence; meanwhile the latter parent may push the child toward more independence and responsibility than he's ready for to compensate for the protective parent. More often it seems that both parents experience both of these feelings at various times and to various degrees; the best scenario is for each parent's extremes to be balanced by the other's more moderate views, but often the synchronization is off.

These disparities are made more complicated by the kid's typically shifting needs: one day she's got everything under control, the next she's ready to quit school and come home to hide. Parents' feelings are mixed, too: You know it's time for your child to move on, but emotionally you're not ready; you're happy he can have the mind-broadening experience of college, but you miss him dreadfully.

The crises often seem to subside gradually as parents get used to the new shape of their everyday lives. Joining a group, going back to school, or becoming immersed in work can be effective ways to defuse a tense situation, which may then resolve itself in a spoken or unspoken compromise. Some couples ignore whatever problems arise and wait for the child's return, when things will go back to the status quo. This is not an ideal solution, since it forces a child to shoulder responsibility for the parents' problems just when she should be learning to be responsible for herself. Other parents are at odds with each other until the child comes home to play peacemaker. This, too, is far from the best way to handle the situation, since the peacemaker child may feel guilty about going back to college and leaving the parents to fight. It's obviously better, if at all possible, for parents to come to some kind of resolution on their own.

Divorced parents may also find that their ways of communicating with each other change. A mother said:

I didn't talk to my ex-husband about our son's roommate problems or about his dropping a course first semester, and my ex didn't ask me about those things. Communication was basically two legs of a triangle—between our son and his dad and between our son and me. I guess if I had a big concern I'd talk to my ex, because I'd think he should know about it, but not about day-to-day things.

Other, more drastic changes may become necessary.

Now that my youngest is at college, I have to sell the house: That was part of the divorce agreement. It will be a little scary, I think—a whole new life for me, too.

One parent summed up the changes in her life when she said, "When your kid leaves for college, it forces you to grow up."

Keeping in Touch

Something that's especially hard for many parents is their lack of day-to-day information about their child's life at college.

> *It was disconcerting—I didn't have any idea of what my son was doing, who he was talking to and what they were talking about; I had no concept of what his days and nights were like. I couldn't picture him: Was he in a classroom or the library or the cafeteria or his room, or somewhere I didn't even know about? It made me feel disconnected and adrift.*

One mother found an innovative way to gather some facts.

> *My older daughter went to visit my younger one at college, and when she got back I asked her about everything I wanted to know, like who are her friends and what does she do socially?—all those things I hadn't seen myself. The answers I got, whether they were true or not, were what I wanted to hear, so I felt much better!*

Not knowing the setting and routine of your kid's daily life can make you feel isolated, out of the loop. But as time goes on, parents often realize that this lack of specific information isn't all bad.

> *I think we worry far less about him when he's at college than when he's home. In a funny way it's out of sight, out of mind. If he's doing something we'd find worrisome, we don't know about it, so we don't get upset—we're unaware of anything to be upset about, and there's nothing we can do about it anyway. It's actually more relaxing for us than having him home.*

Many kids call home frequently in the first few weeks. A phone call every day, or even twice a day, isn't unusual in the beginning. One parent saw his son's frequent calls home as "hidden evidence of the difficulty he was having with separation from the family." A mother said, "My daughter called every day to say hi and that she was miserable."

It's awful to know that your child is unhappy when you want so much for her to love college life. Keep in mind, though, that many kids tend to call home only when they're unhappy. This can be a little misleading; you don't hear from your kid when she's feeling great and on top of things, so you get the idea that she's miserable all the time. In most cases that's not true; it's just that when she's full of energy and enthusiasm, she doesn't need immediate support.

But many parents find that the messages they get from their kids are full of inconsistencies, which can be hard to sort out and make sense of. Parents don't know how to react to the sudden changes in emotional content, and they generally fall into a state of constant worry about their kid's ability to cope.

In the beginning, he was so happy, so I was happy too. But as soon as the unhappiness started to seep in and he let us know he was having some rough days, I got so worried that I wanted to call him every day and see how he was. But I restrained myself. Then he announced that he wanted to transfer! I waited five days and then called and asked if he still wanted to transfer; he said, "No! I love it here." After five days and sleepless nights of worrying! I told him, "Don't ever do that to me again," but I told myself, Don't get sucked into that again. His moods are very up and down, and that's normal, but of course every parent wants their kid to be happy. I didn't expect to be up and down with him so much.

On the other hand, some kids hardly communicate at all. This doesn't necessarily mean they're finding college life smooth sailing. The child who calls twice a day and the child who never calls may be feeling equally confused and homesick. They're just dealing with it differently: One needs frequent infusions of loving contact and support, while the other finds such contact too painful right now and needs to maintain some distance in order not to be overwhelmed with sadness.

E-mail can provide a good solution for a child who's finding the immediacy of phone calls too much to handle. Besides being economical (many colleges have free e-mail hookups for students), it gives him some control and reduces the emotional pressure. He won't have to worry about breaking down in tears when he hears your voice or filling up a long painful pause in the conversation.

> *I never used e-mail before, but now I do. I had the urge to be in touch with my son often, and this is a way that's less intrusive—he's comfortable with it.*

Many families end up communicating almost entirely by e-mail, finding it easy and convenient.

> *My daughter and I e-mailed a lot. It was great. It gave me more sense of her daily life and what she was doing—the little stuff.*

It's important, however, to remember that e-mail isn't always entirely private; there may be some conversations that you, and your kid, would rather not have displayed on a screen where others may read them.

Besides, sometimes you feel you really need to hear your child's voice at the other end of the phone line. In fact, parents' need to talk to their kid is probably just as powerful as the kid's need to talk to them. One father said that he and his wife started a contest to see who was going to be the first to pick up the phone to call their daughter. Another father confessed ruefully that, while his wife was happy with one phone conversation a week, he had been calling their daughter from his office once—and sometimes twice—

every day, and he planned to keep on doing so despite his wife's teasing.

Whatever method of communication you rely on, it's a good idea to discuss it ahead of time. Some families are comfortable with a fairly structured system: a phone call every Sunday at a certain time, for example. Others feel that such a formal arrangement may produce too much stress if their kid forgets to call or has something else to do at that time; they prefer to leave the arrangement more flexible and adapt it as needed.

We talked to our son a lot at first, two or three times a week. That's tapered off—now we talk to him usually once a week. We told him to call us on Sundays because our experience was that when we called him, it was always a bad time—he wasn't in the mood to talk or he had work to do or there were kids in the room, or something. If he calls, he can pick a time that's good for him.

A kid who's feeling a little fragile may not want to talk if roommates and friends are likely to overhear. Remember, too, that your child has a whole life now—of friends, classes, perhaps a job—that's separate from yours; your control of your child's life is lessening, and sometimes a little compromising on both sides helps a lot.

My friend has an only child; when she called and her daughter was busy and couldn't talk at that moment, she'd get very upset. I tried not to do that. If my daughter said she couldn't talk, I accepted it. I knew she had a lot going on and she had to juggle her time the way it worked best for her.

For some kids, it's important to be able to take control of communicating with the family back home.

Our son calls about once a week. It's better to let him call; initiating the calls gives him more independence and more space. You have to let them take the lead.

Another parent had a different slant on the telephone question:

> *When I was in college my parents and I had a formal arrangement: Every Sunday morning at nine, I made a collect call home. But I decided I didn't want my daughter to feel obligated to do that. I wanted her to call when she felt like it; I want her to have contact with me of her own choice as an adult. Also, it's different in a divorce, and I didn't want her to have that burden of being pulled in different directions. So I left it very loose.*

Whether it's loose or structured, communication with your child is important. Kids who seem to have everything under control, as well as those who sound as if they're falling apart, need reassurance from their parents—reassurance that you love them and are proud of them and have confidence in their abilities; reassurance that the first few weeks of college are hard for most students and that things are likely to improve; reassurance that their place in the family is still theirs and that you miss them.

But while you're reassuring your kid, it's hard to know how much of your own feelings to express.

> *When I called my son a few days after we dropped him off, I said, "We miss you so much." There was a pause, and then he said, "Mom, I can't do anything about that."*

Such a response can make you regret your words. You don't want to burden your kid with your problems, and you don't want to make him feel guilty for making you lonely. So you may decide to keep your emotions to yourself. On the other hand, you don't want your child to think you don't miss him at all. A single mother said:

> *When my daughter went to college, I didn't call her often. I didn't want to inflict my problems—of being single and miss-*

*ing her fiercely—on her. Now I wish I'd called more. It would
have made it easier for me, and it wouldn't have hurt her.*

Most kids like knowing they are missed. After all, it's
nice to feel certain that you play an important role at home
and that your absence is noticed.

Finding the right balance for your child may take some
time. For most kids, it's probably better to err on the side
of expressing your feelings than to make it seem his absence
doesn't matter to you, as long as you don't overdo the dramatic sobs. Your child may be tougher than you think. In
addition, it may actually be helpful to a homesick child to
know that his parents are finding the separation difficult,
too; your ability to tell him how you're feeling in a con-
trolled manner, emphasizing your confidence that all of you
will get through this period, provides a model for him in
dealing with whatever unhappiness he's experiencing.

For the first few weeks your phone bill may be enormous. But don't forget to use the mail as well.

*I wrote to my son often—usually not letters, but little notes,
clippings from the newspaper, stuff like that. It didn't matter
what it was, he just liked to get anything in the mail.*

And some parents send lots of packages.

*I sent all kinds of packages—zillions of apples from when we
went apple-picking, a pineapple once, books, pictures, a magazine, just little things; it didn't matter what. I sent funny
cards every week so she got mail—she loved it. I gave her
postcards preaddressed to her grandparents and other relatives;
she sent them, and everyone wrote back. At Parents' Weekend
she opened her desk drawer and said, "Look at all my letters."*

Not every parent can manage this much organization, and
those who don't get around to sending the care packages
they had in mind may feel very guilty about their failings.

It helps to know that some kids don't really want a lot of packages, especially if they're not delivered to the dorms; going to get them at a mail room that's a long walk away and open only at certain times can sometimes feel like a burden instead of a pleasure to a student who's still getting lost on the way to the library.

A good substitute may be a student-run service that delivers birthday cakes and surprise baskets of goodies to assist midterm studying. A student reported:

> *My birthday is in the fall, and my parents were on a business trip in Asia at the time. I thought I'd be kind of sad without even a phone call on my birthday, but then there was a knock on my door and some kid delivered a birthday cake with a message from my mom and dad. It was so nice—it made me feel great! It wasn't very good cake, but it didn't matter what it tasted like.*

And a mother remembered:

> *For my daughter's birthday I had a cake, two plants, and a huge bunch of balloons delivered to her room. I told her in advance to expect a surprise, partly because I wanted to make sure she'd be in her room when it all arrived, but also because I thought the anticipation would be an extra "gift."*

All of these ways of communicating with your kid will probably work for you at different times. What matters most is that your kid knows she can call (or e-mail, or write, or even visit) home whenever she wants or needs to, and that it's okay for her to let you know when she's feeling unhappy. Make sure to keep telling your child that you know the first weeks or months can be very hard and that you're always available with advice, if asked for, or just a sympathetic ear. One parent spoke for many when she said, "The most important thing is to keep your lines of communication always open."

CHAPTER SEVEN

Getting Used to College Life

What's happening to my kid? How is the adjustment to college life going? Is my child doing all right in her courses or on the verge of flunking out? Is he spending the weekends alone in his room or is he out partying all night every night? What about the roommates, and all the other components of my kid's new life?

These questions haunt most parents' minds for the first few weeks after their child goes to college. It's not surprising. Your kid is living in a place you don't know much about, and you feel as if all you can do is hope in a general way that things are going well. One mother summed it up:

> *Your child is making a new identity at college. But the parents aren't there to see it happening; they're not aware of it.*

Sometimes parents catch a glimpse of the new identity, or at least the one their kid is currently trying on for size.

> *My daughter came home on the train for the weekend. When she went back to school, she took dressier clothes—not just the jeans and flannel shirts she wore in high school. I think she feels she can move on now, break out of the mold.*

News—or No News—from the Front

Most parents find it hard to gauge how their kid is doing, especially because from one conversation to the next things often change dramatically. Tremendous enthusiasm about a professor, a roommate, a team sport, or an activity like chorus or theater can turn into disappointment or seeming despair overnight, and sometimes the emotional temperature appears to rise or fall in the space of an hour.

If your kid is the kind who spills out everything she's thinking and feeling, you may find yourself on a roller coaster parallel to hers. When she's full of energy and excitement, you feel great; when she's sobbing and telling you she hates everything about the college, you're overwhelmed with concern—and you feel helpless at the other end of the phone.

Being available when your kid wants to talk, in person or on the phone, is the most helpful thing you can do. Simply acknowledging that this can be a difficult time lets your child know you sympathize, and often that's enough.

But what if your kid isn't telling you much one way or the other? This isn't unusual—some kids reveal very little of what they're doing and how they feel, and many don't like to admit that things aren't going so well. It's easy to feel hurt by this behavior; your child is shutting you out of her new life, not allowing you to be part of it. But kids have understandable reasons for acting this way.

For one thing, they may feel embarrassed or ashamed if they're not completely happy at college. Everyone has been telling them how great it's going to be, and they often feel it's their fault if it's not so great for them. They may wonder "What's wrong with me?," especially if they haven't yet made close friends and everyone else in their dorm and in their classes looks happy and completely on top of things. In addition, kids don't want to disappoint their families; knowing that parents have made substantial financial sacrifices to send them to college often makes kids feel pressured to take advantage of the opportunity without complaint. They may think Mom and Dad will be upset or even angry if they say "I don't know what I'm doing half the time" or "I hate my roommate and everyone in this dorm." So they end up saying only what they think their parents want to hear.

It's disorienting to arrive at a completely new place, go to classes whose content and level of difficulty are still unknown, and live in an unfamiliar room with a total stranger, surrounded by other strangers who are preoccupied with their own problems much of the time. So it's normal for first-year students to be lonely and scared. A kid who is accustomed to hanging out with a group of close friends may find it particularly hard to lose all his support systems in one fell swoop, but even someone who is eager for a new social scene may experience pangs of loneliness on a Saturday evening when she's the only one in the dorm. One student looked back on her first semester:

Sometimes I just wanted to leave. When I felt that way I'd go outside and walk around until I got over it. I had no one to talk to—only acquaintances, no close friends.

Such feelings are sometimes so painful that kids can't admit them even to themselves, much less to their parents.

My son didn't talk much about loneliness until after the fact. By spring semester he could say that the fall had been a rough time for him, but he couldn't say it then. I knew things weren't going well, though, because every time I called he was in his room and I was getting letters from him. Second semester he was never in the room and no letters came, so I knew things were better.

Homesickness is experienced by both sons and daughters, but some researchers have found that boys are far less likely to admit to such feelings than girls. The pattern certainly is not universal, but girls typically talk with their friends, old and new, about being homesick, and they call home to hear their parents' voices, while boys pretend they're doing fine.

This close-mouthed approach makes it even harder for parents to know how to help. But for silent kids as well as the more expressive ones, what matters most is communicating. It helps when you tell your child in general terms that most kids feel confused, lonely, and occasionally depressed, and that you know some of the first experiences at college must be hard to cope with. Acknowledging the likelihood that there will be potholes in the road lets your child know it's okay to admit he's having some problems; encouraging frequent phone calls during this period tells him you're available to talk when he wants to. If he's not ready to discuss his unhappy feelings, you don't have to push him to do so. But a general comment like "It must be pretty hard sometimes to deal with everything" conveys both understanding and confidence that he *can* deal with things, even though it's hard.

Of course it's quite possible that your child, boy or girl, isn't expressing homesickness or unhappiness because it isn't there. Some kids love college life from the start and have only minor downswings to deal with. Parents sometimes find this a little upsetting, as if they think, We're unhappy, so our child should be, too. But try not to insist on problems when there may not be any!

Kids mature at different speeds and respond to stress in different ways, even within families.

My first child was very homesick and very histrionic. She'd call and say how much she missed home, crying on the phone at great length. Then the next day I'd call and it was as if it never happened. With my second, I asked if she was homesick, and she hesitated and then said, "Yeah, a little." She's always been less likely to announce a problem until it's over.

But despite the differences between these sisters, both obviously wanted and needed the phone calls. Letters and cards, too, can provide welcome support and a sense of connection to home without demanding an immediate response.

As the confusion begins to get sorted out and routines are established, parents hear evidence of their children's increasing independence and ability to manage their lives.

> My son called and told me proudly, "I've been successful, I did my laundry." I don't think he's gotten as far as changing the sheets yet, but it seems that doing his laundry made him feel he's taken charge of his life.

By the halfway point of the first semester, many students feel they're finally in control.

> My daughter did well on her midterms, so it's evident that she studies when she's supposed to. Her sleep pattern is bizarre to me; she goes to bed very late and wakes up late because her first class is at 11:00 some days and 1:00 on other days. I'm not too happy about that, but she's comfortable with that schedule. For a while I was worried about the way she was eating—only one meal a day although we were paying for two—but she lost some weight, which she could afford to do, and now she's eating two meals and she's trying to practice good nutrition and avoid the junk. So I think she's managing pretty well.

Learning to handle the details of daily life is an important step toward independence, but kids are learning to manage the larger issues as well. A father recalled:

> We had always done things together as a family, had always taken our daughter wherever she needed to go. After about a month at college she told us, "I suddenly realized I can do anything I want and go anywhere I want; I can basically move around on my own."

Parents can hear the pride in their kids' voices when they recount their steps toward increasing independence. They're discovering that they can make many decisions, large and small, for themselves and that they no longer need their parents to do these things for them.

Such a realization is liberating, but it can also be a little scary for a kid, and you may hear a bit of uncertainty and hesitation in these conversations. It may strike you as perverse that a child who has been eagerly awaiting the chance to be on his own, away from the restrictions and structure of life at home, now occasionally sounds unsure about the idea. But for most kids, progress toward the goal of independence is uneven. They need to turn around and check that the safety net of the family is still in place, and some even need to test the net a bit before moving on again.

Many parents hear another kind of testing when they talk to their college kids, and it's one they've probably heard at earlier stages of the kid's life. Your child may tell you that "everyone" on campus has a car, or drinks all weekend, or takes expensive weekend vacations. Such comments may be her way of asking you for permission to do these things— to drink, to spend money on unsupervised vacations, or to participate in whatever activity is under discussion.

Making decisions about these issues can be complicated. For one thing, you're not there to see if it's true that "everybody" is doing whatever it is or to judge the intensity of peer pressure. Such pressure can be a powerful force, especially for lonely or confused first-year students who desperately want to fit in.

Setting limits for a kid who lives somewhere else isn't easy. But it's helpful to your child if you make your own beliefs and your expectations clear in a matter-of-fact, nonconfrontational way. She may have been hoping, however unrealistically, that you'd say you didn't care if she drank every night. On the other hand, she may have been looking for support in deciding not to drink or just for reassurance that you care a great deal about her and about what she does, even though you're not living in the same place.

It's helpful for divorced parents to try to communicate with each other about these matters.

> *When our daughter has a problem, we let each other know what she says—we've learned to do that. Otherwise we sometimes hear different stories—she can be manipulative. We have a lot of communication. It's very important for her to know that we both love her and that we don't keep things from each other.*

Although you won't necessarily agree about everything, knowing what's going on with the other parent is a big help.

Increasing Independence

Kids are just as aware as parents that the family relationships are beginning to change, and their feelings about it are likely to be mixed, though they may not recognize this. For many, the desire to manage their own lives is accompanied by underlying fears: Will my parents still love me if they don't have to take care of me? Am I hurting their feelings if I don't need their help all the time? Perhaps these fears translate as, Will my parents love me when I'm an adult rather than a dependent child? Most kids still need their parents' approval, even as they test the boundaries of their new freedom. Expressing your pride and confidence in your child goes a long way toward mitigating his concerns— even the ones he's not aware he has.

Many kids also need and want their parents' advice on various specific topics—should they drop a course, join a fraternity, go away for a weekend before an exam? Sometimes they've already made a decision, and they're just checking to see whether your advice confirms it or what your reaction will be.

My son registered for several very hard courses—ones I thought he shouldn't take, at least his first year. We discussed it, but that was his decision. After a couple of weeks he called and left a frantic message—he was dropping the advanced calculus course, was I going to be mad at him?

Other kids seem to go too far in the opposite direction at first. They refuse to ask for advice or help, even when it's clearly appropriate or necessary, sometimes because they need to prove their independence to themselves and sometimes because they think their parents expect them to manage entirely on their own.

Your own feelings about your child's increasing independence are probably somewhat mixed. Of course you're delighted to see her gaining in responsibility and confidence, but at the same time you may feel hurt that you've been pushed aside.

My son was always very independent—never needed help with schoolwork and that kind of thing. But still, I found it very hard when the need to worry about my kid disappeared.

Complicating the situation is the thin line you're trying to tread between running your child's life and withholding advice that might be helpful. Many parents find it works best if they listen to what their child has to say, asking questions that clarify the problem and the possible solutions for themselves and hopefully for the child at the same time. Often advice can be phrased in question form: "Is there a way to talk to your academic adviser about this?" implies a possible action, but it's not as directive and parental-sounding as "I think you should talk to your academic adviser."

Of course, it's not always easy to remain calm and to keep your own emotions under control, but it's definitely worth a try.

Social Life

Adults often look back fondly on their college experience, especially if friendships formed during those years have lasted for several decades. What adults sometimes don't remember is how scary it was at first to find a sea of unknown faces everywhere—in the dorm, in every classroom, in the cafeteria, in the bathroom, even in your own room. One of the best things about college for many people is the chance to get to know a much more diverse group than the friends they had in high school. But the prospect of meeting students from backgrounds entirely different from their own can be a bit daunting for some kids. How will they figure out what to talk about? Will they do or say something irredeemably dumb? Will they even know it if they do?

Part of the problem for many kids is that they've hung out with a small group of close friends in high school and they miss the comfort and camaraderie of that familiar social entity. They are less likely to find this kind of group at college. Even if they end up with a few good friends who do things together, the members of the group are likely to come from different parts of the country and different backgrounds; they won't have the shared experience and culture of a typical high school group.

Kids miss their old friends, yearning for familiar faces and voices all the more because they're trying to adjust to a whole new setting. Some time a visit home to coincide with the high school homecoming game, which provides a chance to touch base with friends. Many keep in close touch with the old gang by phone and especially by e-mail, which is free to students at many colleges.

My daughter called and passed along some gossip about someone we know in our community, which she had found out from a friend's e-mail. I hadn't even heard this news—she was more up-to-date than I was!

You may wonder whether your child's clinging to old friends is such a great idea. Wouldn't he be better off giving himself a chance to make new friends at college? Yes, and he's probably doing that already. But while his new friendships are in the early stages, he may need the comfort of buddies who've known him for a long time and to whom he doesn't have to explain everything. In addition, such friendships can be so strong that kids feel disloyal when they begin making new friends; your child may be e-mailing old friends often just to avoid feeling guilty that they're no longer the only friends in her life.

For most kids, the constant contact with the old group lessens over time, and it's rarely anything that parents need to be concerned about. On the contrary, it can be a big help to kids in the first lonely days and weeks.

Some kids, however, seem to take a long time to find friends at college, and parents worry about what they see as their child's social isolation. It's important to remember that kids aren't all the same, and some of them simply move more slowly than others. A compatible roommate helps a lot, but that's a question of luck. Is there anything you can do to help your kid find some friends?

It's important to step cautiously in this delicate area; you certainly don't want to give the impression that you think your kid is socially incompetent or that you fear no one will want to be friends with him. But you might point out that you've lived a good deal longer than he has and offer suggestions based on your own experience.

One useful approach is to encourage your child to join a group or club that revolves around something he's interested in. Almost anything that provides contact with other people will do. One student looked back on his college experience:

I've always had a hard time in social situations, and for most of the first semester I was pretty lonely. What worked for me finally was finding something outside classes and the dorm to get involved in—I psyched myself up to go to the theater one day and ask someone if I could work backstage. That was where I found people I could make friends with.

Keep in mind, though, that your suggestions may be ignored until later on, when your child feels secure enough about classes and other aspects of his life to branch out in this way.

And what about the high school boyfriend or girlfriend? Plenty of kids hold on to these relationships, too, for many of the same reasons they cling to their old friends. A high school romance is a familiar source of comfort in a new and scary world; it also provides validation—"At least someone loves me, I must be an okay person"; and it's the perfect excuse for a lack of social life at college. Some kids feel even guiltier about "abandoning" their sweetheart than about moving on from old friends, especially if the decision to break up is not mutual.

My daughter was anxious about life without her boyfriend, but she had prepared for it. She misses him, of course, but in some ways she welcomed the end of the relationship because she realized it was time to move on. He wasn't happy about her decision, and that made it very hard for her, but she feels it was the right thing for her to do.

Parents can offer support in general terms for a kid who's ready to explore new relationships. When you tell your child that it's natural and normal to want this freedom in college, that it's rare for high school romances to become permanent commitments, and that dating a variety of people before settling down helps people figure out what they really want in a partner, you provide reassurance, even if clichéd, that it's okay to take advantage of the opportunities in the new social scene. Talking in generalities keeps you outside the danger zone of saying the wrong thing about the not-quite-yet-but-soon-to-be-former relationship or sweetheart, while leaving an opening for your kid to initiate a more personal discussion if wanted.

Another reason for some kids' slow social start in college is that they feel a little scared. Coed dorms can be quite daunting—are you supposed to avert your eyes from or stare at the person returning from the shower clad only in a towel?—and coed bathrooms even more so. In addition, many kids have gone through high school without having a good friend of the opposite sex. Some find the concept strange and confusing, but in coed dorms such friendships are a matter of course. It takes a while for some kids to figure out how they work and to get over their discomfort with the idea.

If a romantic relationship does get started, the combination of coed dorms and no curfews can make it hard to set limits or to let things develop slowly. It's scary when the forward motion seems unstoppable and kids find themselves in bed or close to it with a person they don't yet know very well. Also, modern campus living means kids can spend almost twenty-four hours a day with a boyfriend or girlfriend. They can eat all their meals together, study together in the library or one of their rooms, go out to a lecture or movie together, and, at many colleges, spend the night together. It's more togetherness than some kids want or need at the beginning of a relationship, but there are no rules to provide a convenient excuse for separating. The possibility of too much too soon keeps some students from getting involved at all. This fear of getting in too deep before they're ready may be one explanation for the rise in group dating on many campuses; it's a new take on "safety in numbers," in which surrounding themselves with a group of buddies prevents kids from forming couples.

Parents compare today's freedom with their own college experience and find the difference frightening. It's hard to accept that your kid will have no one to watch what he's doing, no one to make and enforce rules for him, maybe even no one to notice or care if he slides into problems.

News stories about the prevalence of social ills on campus, everything from one-night stands to date rape to sexually transmitted diseases, just increase the tension level.

Many parents take refuge in believing that their kid is mature and smart enough to handle these issues sensibly and safely. It may be wishful thinking—after all, the statistics must represent *somebody's* kids—but it's probably the most pragmatic way to deal with it. Scary though the college social scene may seem, your kid is going to have to cope with it on her own. The preparation for life that you've already given her is what she'll rely on, along with your, and her own, confidence in her ability to make appropriate choices.

If she does want to talk about a problem in this area, it helps if you can discuss it calmly and pay attention to the cues she gives you. Pressing for specific information before a child is ready to provide it can simply shut down the communication; telling her what to do won't work as well as asking what she sees as her options and pointing out aspects she may not have considered. Stating your views is important, because your child may be looking for support and reassurance that she's doing the right thing. But it's wise to state them as your views—"You know I've always believed that . . ."—rather than as commands. This allows your kid to decide to agree with you, which is much easier than obeying you.

The Commuter Student's Perspective

The adjustment process isn't that much easier for kids who are commuting to college, or for their parents. You may find that because you see your child every day, you're very aware of his anxiety and distress, but there's not a lot you can do to make things better. He's going off every day to a group of people you don't know and a system you have no power to change. And he may resent any attempt you make to find out what's troubling him.

Many commuter students, perhaps precisely because they are still living at home under their parents' eyes, seem to erect an impenetrable wall between home and school. They need to make their college world theirs alone, and a parent's interest and concern is often interpreted as "trying to run my life." This is difficult for parents, who can't help wanting everything to go smoothly and perfectly for their kids. But at least at first, you'll probably create less friction if you keep your comments and questions very general. Saying "I bet everyone in your class is still feeling pretty confused and anxious" may spark a conversation about your child's uncertainties; if not, you've at least let him know you'll lend a sympathetic ear if he needs one.

It may seem strange, but students who live at home often feel as "homesick" as those who live on campus. Though they haven't moved away, they usually have less contact with their parents than they had in high school, and they are expected to be much more independent now that they're in college. Like their peers in residential colleges, boys usually find it harder than girls do to admit to this kind of "homesickness" for the way things used to be.

But for many students, such feelings don't last long, and their new independence quickly becomes a source of increased self-confidence. The father of a commuter student said:

The courses he chose at first didn't all work out. It was too hard to come home and then go back for the evening course, so he dropped that one and switched to a different course that he's much happier with. It was his decision to do it. He wants to do things on his own, and he's worked out a method: His whole life, everything he needs, is in his car, because that way he knows he won't forget anything.

Even if you sometimes smother a sigh at your child's inefficient or tortuous ways of reaching decisions, you no doubt feel proud and happy as you see her stretching her wings. But your kid's newly adult behavior may also make you nostalgic for the old days. A mother said:

> I expected things to remain more the same, not realizing how much she'd be branching out and doing her own things. Even though she's still living at home, there's not the same dependency. It's withdrawal time for me.

If your kid attends a nonresidential college close to your home, some of her high school classmates are likely to be there, too. This often raises concerns for parents; when high school buddies attend the same commuter college they often continue to stick together, especially if they carpool to the campus. It's convenient and comfortable, but you may worry that it's keeping them from making new and perhaps more mature friendships and from taking advantage of the larger pool of potential soulmates.

Try to remind yourself that, at the beginning, your kid may need the security of tried and true friends as she enters a new environment. But it's unlikely that she'll have the same schedule and the same courses as her buddies, so she'll be encouraged to branch out and meet new people. If you're concerned that your child seems to be clinging too firmly to the old crowd, you might suggest that she get involved in an extracurricular activity of some kind; sports, political groups, and charitable organizations all offer interesting possibilities. It takes longer for some than for others, but eventually most commuter students acquire a social group that's both varied and wide-ranging.

When Your Kid Is Unhappy

By the time a few weeks have passed, most kids feel fairly well settled at college. They know their way around the campus, they've made some friends, they've begun to feel that they understand how things work, and they've figured out how to manage their time and their studies to some extent. Some, though, may continue to feel unhappy.

Often, even if they think they will want to transfer, they make up their minds to stick it out for the first year or the first semester, rather than dropping out now. Parental pressure sometimes encourages this decision.

> *We had talked about what my son thought it would be like to be in college, and I told him the adjustment isn't always easy. But I said he had to go through one whole year before he could decide he couldn't stay there, because it takes a while to get used to anything.*

Money enters the discussion for most families. When a kid threatens to drop out of school, parents see a semester's payments washed down the drain, and they may resent the child's obliviousness to this substantial loss. The same is true if the kid appears to be goofing off and in danger of flunking out; it's hard not to feel upset when your financial sacrifices seem to be ignored or brushed aside. At the other end of the spectrum, parents may worry that their child's part-time job, though providing financial help, is taking too much time away from his studies.

Conflicts between parents, on this and other issues, may reflect their different expectations: One may expect the kid to focus on studying and getting good grades to prepare for a good job after college, while the other may expect the child to indulge in a busy social life, accompanied by adequate grades. Parental responses may also reflect other issues. For example, telling a child to give up her part-time job will make her more dependent financially on her parents, and that may be a way of keeping her emotionally dependent as well.

Talking to other parents is often a good way to gain some perspective on how concerned you should be. It's extremely reassuring to hear that other kids are going through similar difficulties, and it's helpful to find out how other parents are handling things. Of course, only you can determine your own child's needs. But comparing your situation with others' can provide a chance to step back and think about it calmly. It can also help both parents agree on a course of action and avoid giving conflicting messages to the child, who has enough to contend with at the moment.

Serious Problems and Difficult Decisions: How to Help Without Taking Over

Naturally, all parents hope their kids will sail through college easily and smoothly. But sometimes problems arise that require your help. A kid may have serious difficulties with a roommate, for example, or with alcohol or drug issues.

Often you'll find that talking things over leads to a resolution, so it's important to stop yourself from jumping in immediately with advice or instructions. Be aware that she may have already made a decision and is hoping for your confirmation that it's a good one or simply for your support in a difficult situation.

> It was obvious from the beginning that my son's roommate would be difficult because he had a drug problem. I had to reassure my son that it was okay to say, "No, you can't do drugs here, it's my room as well as yours." You want to constantly reassure your child that it's all right to keep to his own standards, his own values, no matter what the roommate wants.

Even if you don't at first agree with your kid, try to take a step back and think it over from his point of view: perhaps you'll conclude that what would be the right decision for an adult is not the best choice for a college freshman. A student described how she handled a roommate problem:

> *Things got so bad that I'd come back to the room and see her
> there and just turn around and leave, but I decided to stick
> it out. I have a friend who hated her roommate and went to
> her RA [resident adviser] about it; she moved to another floor
> of the dorm, and she was fine. But I think what I did was
> also fine. It might have been better if I'd chosen to move, but
> at the time I didn't feel ready to go and introduce myself to
> a whole new group of people and start over again. I think if
> you can talk things out, you should, but if not, you just have
> to find somewhere else to study because you only have to use
> your room for sleeping.*

This girl's solution was not necessarily the one her parents
would have chosen, but it worked for her. It also demon-
strated that she could deal with a problem successfully in
her own way, which is a great confidence-builder.

When a kid continues to sound sad and unenthusiastic
as time goes on, parents may wonder if he's depressed. Certainly some students, especially freshmen, do get depressed.
They seem to take longer than others to adjust to a new
environment and establish a new support system of friends
and advice-givers. They may also be having trouble adjusting to a new image of themselves; a kid who's been at
the top of his class all along may now be one of many high
school valedictorians and may be struggling for the first time
in his life to get decent grades. Such a change can foster a
lot of self-doubt and loss of confidence.

For many kids, getting through this unhappy phase is a
matter of time; by second semester he may have a better
grasp of the academic work and at least the beginnings of
a group of friends. In the meantime, it's important for you
to keep in touch with him.

When talking things over doesn't appear to be enough,
try suggesting sources of help for your kid on campus. The
college probably sent a list of who is available for what
kinds of problems—including the RA on your child's dorm
floor, tutors for help with courses, your child's adviser, the

freshman dean, the college health services, and everything in between. But some kids are reluctant to make use of these resources, maybe because they're unwilling or scared to admit they need help. Others just can't seem to get it together to figure out what's available, since the whole system is unfamiliar.

In either case, reminding your kid that help is there for the asking is often useful; you might point out that going to a teacher's office hours for clarification shows that a student cares, and that most teachers are thrilled when students make use of the opportunity. Tell your child, too, that getting the perspective of someone who knows a lot about the problem will provide more information, and it doesn't commit your kid to accepting the adviser's solution. You might suggest, too, that your kid talk to an older student—perhaps she's gotten to know some sophomores or juniors in her dorm or in one of her classes. It can be very helpful for a confused freshman to talk over a problem with someone who has recently been there.

It's tempting to try to solve your kid's problems yourself. But this is a temptation to be resisted. An elementary school teacher said:

> My neighbor's niece, who's a senior, didn't like her student teaching placement, so she had her dad call the dean and complain. This is the kind of thing I tell parents of elementary school kids is inappropriate, and it's still going on in college! So I wasn't surprised that when my son dropped a course in organic chemistry, people kept telling me I shouldn't have let him do it. I told them, "I didn't 'let' him, and he didn't ask me." It was his decision. I think that's what he's supposed to do in college—make his own decisions—but I find a lot of people don't agree with me.

If you rush to visit your kid whenever he sounds upset or you storm into the administrative office to demand action, you risk implying that you think your child can't manage without you to help him. Before you even pick up the phone, remember that part of what parents want their kids to get from college is the independence and maturity that come from making one's own decisions—and also one's own mistakes. And this can happen only if you let go of the reins.

On the other hand, you don't want to make your kid think you don't care what happens. Let her know you're concerned, and follow up on conversations to see if things have gotten better. And continue to express your confidence in your child's ability to handle the problem responsibly.

It's not easy to find the balance between taking charge and backing off altogether, and it's definitely not easy for most parents to acknowledge that their kid is becoming an adult. But it's exciting as well, and since it's going to happen in any case, you might as well look at the positive side of it.

I just talked to a woman who said, "I'm not going to let my daughter do this or that when she's in college." And I said to her, "Once she's there, you're not going to be able to do anything about it." I think that's the most important piece: recognizing that this is your child's next step away from you. And you have to be able to admit that for you it's both a happy and a sad step.

CHAPTER EIGHT

Together Again for the First Time

Parents' Weekend

Parents' Weekend—it's something you've been looking forward to with eager anticipation. Perhaps you haven't seen your child since freshman orientation; even if your kid has come home for a weekend, you haven't seen the campus with college life in full swing. The opportunity to observe your kid in the physical context of her new life makes everything much more concrete and real.

> *I was glad I went and saw my daughter in her daily life at college. It makes it easier when you can really visualize what your kid is telling you about on the phone.*

But the main purpose of Parents' Weekend for most parents is reassurance; they want to see their child settled into her new space, to meet her new friends, to see for themselves that she's comfortable and at home there. And most parents come away with their need for reassurance satisfied. However, the weekend itself may be somewhat different from what they expect.

Even for a kid who seems happy and secure at college,

having parents on campus may create some awkwardness.
A father described the weekend:

> *It was very pleasant; our son seemed relaxed and at home,
> with lots of friends. He enjoyed showing us around campus
> on Saturday and going out to eat. But after dinner he was
> anxious to leave us and go to a fraternity party. The next day
> he apologized and said maybe we should have come with him
> to the party! He was obviously a little uncertain about what
> we should do while we were there and, although he was happy
> to see us, he worried about taking care of us.*

It's typical for both parents and kids to feel slightly
askew, as if the pieces aren't fitting together quite right.
Parents don't know their way around and have to wait for
their kid to show them where to go, to take them into the
dining hall for lunch and explain where the salad bar is, to
direct them to the sites of any events they want to attend.
This is a reversal of roles, and after many years of being in
charge, many parents find it a bit unsettling, though their
kids may enjoy the feeling of competence and superior
knowledge.

In addition, parents most likely don't know any of the
other parents who are there for the weekend. In some ways
this may be a good thing, because it gives parents a small
taste of what the first few weeks of college were like for
their child, but it also has the effect of making them entirely
dependent on their kid for company and conversation.

> *It was a little odd. By this time in our daughter's life, we
> don't normally spend twelve hours face-to-face or eat three meals a
> day with her. It was great to see her; we loved the fact that she
> seemed happy and had made such a good adjustment, but after
> dinner we let her go out with her friends and didn't need to
> see her again. She was happy to be with us, but I think also
> happy when we left.*

Joining forces with a roommate's parents can help reduce the intensity of constant contact. Of course, this depends on two pieces of luck—that your kid gets along with the roommate, and that you get along with the roommate's parents. When it works, it's great.

Parents' Weekend started out a little awkwardly—our daughter didn't seem very pleased to see us, and she kept saying she had a lot of work to do so she couldn't go with us to any of the program events. But then her roommate showed up with her parents, whom we had met and liked in September. The two girls immediately started talking to each other, ignoring the adults, but it was okay because all of us parents went to the speeches and arranged to meet the girls for lunch. By that time our daughter seemed a little less tense, and the six of us had a really nice time. Having other parents there besides us obviously took the pressure off for her.

Still, whether you hook up with other parents or not, you may feel just a bit hurt when your kid clearly doesn't need you to be around. It's even worse if you get the feeling that your kid doesn't *want* you on campus. But for some kids, it's important to keep their two lives as separate as possible. A first-year student said:

I didn't have time to see them on Parents' Weekend, and I told them that—I said I'm going to be in rehearsals all day Saturday, and Saturday night you won't see me. But they came anyway. It was tricky, there was nothing for them to do most of the time. It's strange to have parents come—two totally different worlds mixed together.

It's easy to feel annoyed (you didn't come all this way to *not* see what your child is doing at college), and it's even easier to feel insulted if your kid seems to hustle you away from social interactions and fails to introduce you to his friends. Do your best not to be hurt—acting this way is very common!—and try to look at it from your kid's standpoint. His behavior doesn't mean he's embarrassed to acknowledge you. Instead, he probably doesn't feel secure enough yet in the college setting to risk seeing it through your eyes. He's worried about what you will think, and your anticipated criticism—of a roommate, of the neatness or lack thereof of the dorm room, of the weekend's planned events, even of the college food—will be hard for him to handle, because he isn't certain yet of his own feelings and evaluations. So he has to keep you at arm's length from "his" college for a while. This is his life, and he has to find his own way of dealing with it, since his parents have no role in it; but it may be too early for him to feel comfortable in exposing his decisions and compromises to his parents.

No doubt you have no intention of criticizing, but you may not be given the opportunity in any case. Lots of kids see Parents' Weekend as a time to get away from campus completely.

> *She showed us around and everything, but then she said, "Let's do as much away from here as we can." She stayed with us both nights in the hotel and wanted to spend as much time with us as possible. We hardly spent any time on campus, although there were lots of things going on—she made it clear that's what she wanted.*

This choice isn't unusual, even for kids who seem happy and involved in the college scene. As first-year students, they're still learning their way around both physically and mentally, and a weekend away from the pressure to get things right is a chance to take off the armor and relax in the company of people who know them well and love them warts and all. Looking at it that way, you can see its irresistible appeal, especially since it also serves to keep college and home separate from one another. This need to compartmentalize the two streams of life is strongest now, near the beginning of a student's first year. By the second year, most kids are able, often eager, to welcome parents into their college world.

Since the Parents' Weekend experience varies greatly, it's probably best to let your kid take the lead in deciding what to do. If he needs time to study, you can attend the planned events for parents; if he clearly wants time alone with you off campus, you can skip the parents' events without compunction. But whatever your child's choices about how to spend the weekend, one thing seems universal—he will want to go out to dinner.

> *They all want to go out to dinner on Parents' Weekend. You need to make reservations way ahead, especially in small towns; we didn't know that, and we drove all over before we found a restaurant that had space for us. We wanted to take him somewhere nice, not just for fast food—we wanted it to feel like a special occasion.*

It's best, too, to let your kid take the lead in deciding whether to invite a roommate, especially one whose family isn't there, to share any part of the weekend. Even if the roommate is a good friend by now, your kid may prefer to get away from college entirely so he can feel free to talk completely openly with you. On the other hand, sharing some parts of the festivities with another student, with or without family, can be a lot of fun and can also give you a broader picture of your child's everyday life.

Who goes to Parents' Weekend can become a major issue for divorced parents. One mother said:

> *My ex and his wife went up for Parents' Weekend—he was insistent that they were going. So I decided I'd stay home. I thought the last thing my daughter needed was to have all three of us trailing her around and making her nervous and uncomfortable. But I felt bad about not going, so I went up to see her the next weekend.*

This kind of solution works for many families. Especially during your kid's first year at college, it's a good idea to avoid adding extra pressures to what she's already experiencing. If you can figure out a way to divide the visits to and from college so that no one feels left out or cheated, you'll all feel more cheerful.

What do you do if you realize, upon arriving for Parents' Weekend, that your kid is really unhappy at college? You probably knew already that things weren't going perfectly for him, but seeing you in person may prompt him to say that he's so miserable he wants to drop out.

First, try not to panic. You'll no doubt experience conflicting feelings in your reaction to this bombshell. In addition to the financial loss that dropping out will cause, many parents feel that "quitting" is something to be ashamed of, especially if all the other kids they know seem to be having the time of their lives. So a child who says he hates the college and doesn't feel happy there may feel pressure from his parents to stay.

Yet this isn't always the worst approach. Dropping out midsemester can make a child feel like a failure, no matter how much you say he's not. More significantly, it's hard to judge the seriousness of the situation. A kid who is miserable in October may very well be much more relaxed and comfortable by December; and for many, the experience of coping successfully with problems creates a sense of personal growth and increased self-confidence.

A weekend spent mainly off campus with you may be all your kid needs to feel better about facing the rest of the semester. Talk about what's making him unhappy, discuss possible steps to improve the situation, express sympathy, and, most important, reiterate your faith in his ability to find a way to cope.

In addition, if you feel the problems may never be resolved satisfactorily, suggest that he talk to his adviser and look into the possibilities for transferring, either after the first semester or at the end of the year. Sometimes knowing that transferring is an option and finding out how to go about it takes the pressure off the current situation, and that may be enough to reduce the problems to manageable proportions.

Whatever the outcome of your Parents' Weekend, it's an opportunity to see your child living and working in a new setting that belongs to her and not to you and a fascinating chance to watch her start to integrate her old and new lives.

First Visit Home

If your kid isn't too far away, it's likely that he'll come home for a visit during the fall—perhaps the long Columbus Day or Veterans Day weekend or maybe not until Thanksgiving. Whenever it is, you probably can't wait to see him. You've missed him and his familiar presence in the house, and you look forward to having the family together again at home.

Early signs of his impending arrival may begin a day or two before he gets home. You may notice that the phone is ringing more often than usual, as his old friends call to see when he'll get there or to announce where the group is going to meet. These calls remind you of how much your child's presence at home affects your life, and soon you're anticipating all the other signs that he's in residence—the pile of sneakers in the hall, the increased noise level in the house, the crumbs on the kitchen counter after he and his friends have found something to snack on.

But if it's at all possible, try not to let the glow of anticipation get too bright, because often a kid's first visit home from college doesn't live up to expectations. To everyone's surprise and dismay, it may be stressful, difficult, and disappointing for you and for your kid. How can that be? you wonder. But when you think it over, it makes sense.

If your child is happy at college, adjusting well and enjoying the freedom and the responsibility, home may seem pretty tame and boring.

Our daughter came home for a weekend—just walked in and surprised us. We were so happy to see her, and she was happy to see us, especially the dog—she spent the first hour playing with her. During the weekend she was out a lot; I didn't actually see that much of her, but her closest friends weren't home and she said, "It's so boring here." She went up to the high school, but she felt out of place, not comfortable. Her brother was excited to see her, but within half an hour they were back to their old bickering. By Sunday she couldn't wait to get "home" to college.

Another parent explained things this way:

After a weekend home, he couldn't wait to get back to school. It's a revelation for him to be in a place where nobody's telling him what to do. We're fairly strict, and we're always asking him questions—have you done this, did you remember that? It's an amazing experience for him to be totally on his own, and he loves it.

Such a weekend hits you over the head with the realization that your kid has another life somewhere else and that his old life doesn't fit him in the same way it used to. You may feel hurt, rejected, and redundant—your child doesn't need you anymore.

When my son was home for a three-day weekend, I kept trying to make food he would love. I said, "I'll cook this, I'll cook that," and finally he said, "What are you doing? Let me alone." But I felt I just had to make everything perfect so he'd have a good time at home—it was tense.

It's not fun to feel unappreciated. And when your kid spends the whole visit sleeping until noon or later and then, after a quick forage through the fridge, going out with whichever old friends he can find and coming home at three in the morning, you can start to feel pretty annoyed. When is he going to have time to sit down and talk with you, tell you how he's doing, fill you in on his classes, his roommates, his social life?

But it looks a little different from your kid's point of view. She needs to touch base with all of her old life, not just her family, to make sure it's still there for her. In fact, her "ignoring" you may be evidence that she feels secure and accepted at home—she knows her family still loves her, so she doesn't have to spend time making sure that it's true, which is actually a wonderful compliment if you can see it that way. Also, she's probably not yet completely comfortable at college and she may want this weekend to be a brief escape, a time-out. A student said:

My dad asked a million questions when I was home. I had come back for a break, but it felt like he was saying, "We can't talk about anything else except how is college going." It made things harder—what can you say when someone asks direct questions like that all the time?

Another said:

My first weekend home, everyone wanted to know all about college, and I felt I had to lie and pretend I was having a great time, which I wasn't yet. It was hard. And it was also hard going back afterward because school wasn't really home yet.

If your child is able and willing to tell you about his life at college—his friends, his classes, this teachers—enjoy it and be grateful that you're getting to hear so much. Try not to interrupt the flow. A father said:

Don't offer too much of your own experience—try to avoid the temptation to tell too many stories about your own college years. It's better to listen more, recognizing that your kid is going through one of the most amazing changes of his life.

Some kids seem to have no problems at all readjusting to home. If this is the case, consider yourself lucky—and be prepared to miss your kid all over again when he leaves.

There was no need to adjust when he came home—we just slipped right back into the same old routines. We were happy to see him, he was happy to be home. But when he left, it was like reliving the first leaving in September—it hadn't gotten easier.

But many parents find that in the few short weeks since their kid left for college, they've developed a slightly different set of routines, and a visit from the child causes a minor disruption. A mother of two college students said:

I love having both kids under the roof, the whole family is here together. But I worry more when they're here. I make them wake me up when they come in, so if they're out late I don't sleep well. I think they're coming home for dinner, so I fix food, and then they call and say they're not coming—it's chaos. So I'm very happy to have them home for a visit, but not unhappy to have them go back.

A visit home plays out differently for a kid who's not happy about her life at college, and parents are likely to feel upset and helpless.

There was a lot of tension when our daughter came home for a weekend. As it got close to time for her to leave, she sat down and talked to us in a very negative, angry way—she hates it, the people are horrible, she didn't want to go back. I'm not sure she'd feel any different about anywhere else, but she sounded so resentful. We felt stabbed in the heart. I cried a lot. My husband was better; he talked things through with her, and at least she listened and maybe took away a grain of advice that would help her make it through.

When you hear your child express so much unhappiness and pain, you may feel guilty that you're throwing her back into the lions' den. But unless you think she's so overwhelmed that she's in danger of doing something really self-destructive, it's probably best to harden your heart and send her back to work things out for herself. Remember that many kids go through both highs and lows in the first few months of college, and as her parent you're more likely than anyone else to see the lows, because she trusts you to sympathize and understand. Making sure she knows you have confidence in her abilities is the best help you can provide right now.

You may be surprised by other sources of friction that can make this first visit home a stressful time. For example, rearrangements of their living space can upset kids quite a lot.

After my son left for college, I moved some of his stuff in order to create more storage space. The first time he came home he had a fit—it was his room and I'd changed it. As if his welcome home depended on what was in his room.

Keep in mind that kids have looked forward to coming home to their safe space, and they've imagined it exactly the way it was when they left. Certainly it's not necessary to turn your child's room into a shrine, but rearranging his living space the minute he's out the door feels to him as if you couldn't wait to get rid of him.

We don't have a lot of extra room, and I decided to make my daughter's room into an office and move her in with her sister. But when I told her my plans on the phone, she was really mad at me. She said, "Can't you at least let me keep my room until I come home for Thanksgiving? Let me sleep there one more time before you throw me out." I had no idea she'd feel so strongly about it.

No matter how logical your reasons are for the changes, your kid may feel both bereft and angry. So, if you can, wait until the first semester, or even the first year, is over before you make radical changes. By that time your child is likely to be able to accept them much more readily and may even enjoy helping plan the new arrangement.

Changes in the family that's still home, though, aren't so easy to postpone. When a child leaves home, especially an oldest child, the younger siblings often seem to move up to take new positions in the family. Then, when the oldest comes home, he may feel excluded and unwelcome.

When our son came home for five days at Thanksgiving, it was very unpleasant. It was the first time he'd been home and we'd all been together, and I think there was a lot of anxiety and nervousness for all of us. At one point, it wasn't intentional, but my husband and I and the three younger kids were in the living room, crowded together on the couch, and he came in and said, "Ah, there's the happy little family." We had needed to huddle together for a moment, but until he said that, we didn't realize that's what we were doing. I think we had just gotten settled into the new family configuration, and then he came back and changed it.

Of course you feel terrible if your kid feels left out and excluded, but the fact is that the family has changed to adjust to his not being there, and in some ways he's happy about that. On one level he's pleased to be growing more independent and dipping his feet into the currents of adulthood; when he says snappishly that he's not in high school anymore and he doesn't have to keep a curfew at college so why should he have to at home, he's saying he's moved on from the former family structure. But on another level he probably wants to be enfolded in the family embrace and to abandon his responsibilities for a few days.

Just as it's hard for your kid to balance the old and new roles, it's hard for you to know how much to loosen the parental reins. After all, even though he's in college, he's still a teenager. Should you forget about curfews and expect not to know where he is or when he'll be back?

> *On his first visit home, our son went out with his friends on Friday night, saying he'd be back by two o'clock. We went to sleep around midnight, and when I woke up at six in the morning, he wasn't home. It was too early to call and see if he'd slept over at a friend's house, so I paced for two hours, imagining wrecked cars and fatal muggings, until I could start phoning. Of course it turned out he was at a friend's, so I made them wake him up. I was so angry at him, but he kept saying, "I'm sorry, I forgot to call, I don't have to call anyone when I'm at school."*

It's true that at most colleges, students don't have many restrictions and rules to be concerned about. Still, when your kid is home, it's fair to expect that he'll be considerate of you and the rest of the family; point out to him that a phone call to allay your concern and keep you from worrying is what a responsible adult would do.

And sometimes you can't keep from behaving like a mother hen who needs to protect her child in the big bad world.

> *My daughter took the bus for her first trip home, so I went to pick her up at the downtown station. I'd never been there before, and when I saw how big and confusing it is, I was so scared for her. I got there a little late and I couldn't figure out if her bus had arrived or not. They were so rude at Information, no one helped, and then some guy said that bus had arrived a couple hours before. I was terrified, I couldn't move, I just stood there frozen. Then I called home in case somehow she had gotten there, but she hadn't. So I just waited. At last the bus came, two hours late, and three or four other buses came at the same time. I didn't know which one she was on, I was running from one to the other like a crazy person, and*

*when at last I saw her get off a bus, I hugged her and refused
to let her go. She was embarrassed—she couldn't understand
what my problem was.*

An experience like this crystallizes the conflicting emotions that parents often feel: the fierce desire to take care of your child and protect her from harm, and the helpless realization that she's moving into the wider world over which you have little control. You can't be there to hold her hand as she crosses the street anymore, and that's a bittersweet acknowledgment to make. Having your kid home for a few days may bring these emotions to the surface, making it hard for you as well as your child to find your footing in a relationship with new parameters.

For divorced parents, a child's first visit home can present other kinds of problems. Who decides which parent the child will stay with for this brief time? Whether it's the parents' or the child's decision, it's difficult to avoid hurt feelings and miscommunication. A father said:

*My son's first visit home was very tense because my ex-wife
wanted to go up and meet him for a minivacation near the
college. I knew our son planned to come home, so I told my
ex to call him and discuss it. But she said, "No, he has to
call me if he wants to talk about it." But since our son didn't
know about the minivacation idea, he didn't call his mother.
So then I had to call him and explain and tell him to call his
mom, which he did. It worked out that he came home and
spent some time with each of us, but the whole thing was
uncomfortable and everyone was sort of upset. It's a problem
figuring out who he stays with and how much time he spends
where—it's not so easy.*

For some families, a simple agreement that the child will spend equal time with both parents works out well. However, that can be difficult to arrange when parents live far apart, and the kid may object to being shipped off to another part of the country when he wants to have time to reconnect with his high school friends and revisit familiar places. On the other hand, leaving the decision up to the kid can be tricky.

> *All through high school we arranged for our daughter to split her vacations fifty-fifty between our two households—we wanted to free her from having to choose one or the other of us. But when she went to college, she was worried because suddenly she wasn't free from making those decisions. She said once, "How am I going to do that?" And I told her, "You can keep on doing everything fifty-fifty, but I want the choice to come from you; I don't want to lock you into a formula." She'll be an adult soon, and I want her to spend time with me because she wants to, not because she has to.*

For some kids, making these choices and coping with concerns about hurting the feelings of one parent or the other may be too much of a burden, while for others it can be a welcome acknowledgment of their increasing maturity. In families where hostility between the divorced parents lingers, a formal agreement on this and other issues may be the best solution. No one approach works for all families, but keeping the focus on the child's needs rather than the parents' can often defuse the situation.

What if your kid wants to bring his roommate or a friend home with him? This is quite likely, especially at Thanksgiving, if you live near the college and the friend's family is far away. You'll no doubt feel guilty if you say no; you'll be imagining your kid's friend alone in the dorm on a day whose traditions include welcoming strangers and gathering together in celebration. And you hope that if your kid were in that position, someone would invite him to share their family holiday.

Still, especially if this will be your kid's first visit home, you may not want to share this precious time with him, no matter how selfish that seems. A friend you've never met will change the dynamics, and you may fear you won't have a chance to reestablish the intimate family circle.

If at all possible, though, stifle your doubts and welcome your kid's friend as warmly as you can. Keep in mind that this quick visit might not be all you want it to be anyway, even if your kid came home alone. Remember, too, that your child will be grateful and proud of his family for extending a sense of home to his friend. It's a way to strengthen the connections between the two environments your child inhabits.

But what if your kid doesn't want to come home?

We always have Thanksgiving with friends and their fami-
lies—lots of people. But my daughter didn't come home for
Thanksgiving her first year; she spent it with a couple of
friends who also weren't going home. It was her decision—
she needed to feel independent that first year.

How can you help not feeling hurt by such a decision, not to mention the awkwardness of explaining to family and friends why your child has made this choice? Probably you can't. But your kid's need to test her ability to manage on her own may be a powerful one, and you can take comfort in the fact that her sense of security with her family is strong enough that she doesn't have to come home to make sure it's still intact. Besides, from Thanksgiving it's not long until the December vacation and semester break.

By now you may be thinking that your first visit with your kid after he's left for college is something to be dreaded. Of course that's not the case. Your first glimpse of him is likely to create a tremendous rush of parental love and pride, and your pleasure in talking with him about his college experiences is enhanced by the growth and increased maturity you see in him. But knowing that there may be a few missteps as you reestablish contact may help you take them in stride.

CHAPTER NINE

Living at Home Again: Coping with and Enjoying Changes

Winter Break

For most kids, December brings their first long visit home. If the college is on a semester plan, this vacation may stretch through most of January to include the semester break. Both kids and parents look forward to it eagerly—they anticipate a relaxed and festive atmosphere, with plenty of chances to spend time together without feeling rushed. A mother described her feelings:

What was Christmas vacation like? It was wonderful—the hole was no longer empty. For the first time in a long while there was a feeling of being a complete family. It was a pleasure to have her here—we laughed, she talked a lot, we were able to relax.

Parents are sometimes amazed at the changes in their kids since the beginning of the semester. They seem to have grown up a lot in a short time, and they are more independent and self-sufficient. They've completed a semester, and their sense of accomplishment and mastery is evident.

My son seemed so different from when he left in August. In those four months he matured incredibly. There were a lot of

148

unsettling times for him and for us during that period, but by Christmas everything had fallen into place; he'd made his niche, he got over his loneliness and began to develop a comfort level. It's obvious that college is where he needs to be right now—it's his time.

A kid's newfound maturity sometimes emerges in ways that surprise parents.

My daughter never read for pleasure in high school—she didn't even read all the books she was supposed to for class. But when she was home for Christmas she read a book that she'd used Cliff Notes *for in her senior year. She said, "This is a great book. I can't believe how stupid I was in high school not to take advantage of everything." She talked a lot about how in high school there were so many courses she half listened to, so many books she didn't read. She said, "I just did what I had to to get by, but now I'm so excited about my courses, I love to read."*

Such a change in perspective can be tremendously exciting for parents, too. But of course your kid's greater sense of independence can also create a bit of friction. Meshing your lives smoothly again can be tricky, and you can end up at odds over insignificant details.

My daughter went back to school after the vacation with dirty clothes because she chose not to get up early that last day and do laundry. But she wouldn't let me get near any of that. I offered to wash the clothes for her, but she said no. It's a territorial issue now, I guess, and the minute I get near it, there's tension.

It's often difficult for a kid who's been away to accept your rules and restrictions. One parent said, "It's the parents' problem—they worry if the kid is out late or doesn't call. But to the kid it feels like squeezing into a shoe that's too small." Another recalled:

> *Over semester break our son wanted to drive about a hundred miles in a snowstorm to visit a friend from college, and he was very angry when we didn't let him go. The tension comes when we start to act like parents. He's so used to being away from us and having no one tell him what to do or put any limits on him, that when we start to make rules or worry about him, it's hard. He feels like he can fly, but we're still not quite ready to let him fly.*

There's no question that it's hard for a kid to feel hemmed in when he's used to being free to make his own rules. But it's hard for you, too. Enforcing your rules may make you feel like the bad guy; you don't want your kid to be angry and frustrated the whole time he's home, and you do want to acknowledge that he's more mature and responsible now and therefore the old rules may be outdated. Yet at the same time you probably feel that living at home as a family requires everyone to agree to some rules that make life easier.

> *The vacation was hectic because our daughter wanted to spend so much time with her old friends. They were going from one house to the other, it seemed she was out till five A.M. every night, so we didn't see much of her. It was frustrating, but at the same time I knew some good stuff was happening with her and her friends, and that was important to her.*
>
> *However, there were some things we demanded, like having Sunday dinner together, making a point of all being home for dinner another night, having a family evening at the movies. But we had to plan ahead, not just say in the morning that we wanted her home for dinner tonight. We can't depend on her being free around our schedule, the way it was when she was in high school.*

In addition, there will be times when you feel that however mature your kid may be at college, at home he slides right back into a less responsible mode. He's no doubt enjoying the relaxation, but as you pick up his dirty clothes and rinse his unwashed dishes for the twentieth time, you may think you'd better go back to the rules you had when he was ten.

Planning ahead helps a lot, and so does making your expectations clear about family time together. It may take a little while for your child to fit back into the family constellation and adjust to the altered family dynamics. But it's also important for you to recognize the changes in your kid and to allow a good deal of flexibility in the rules. The more openly you discuss these issues with your child, the less friction is likely to arise, and your child will appreciate being treated more like the adult he or she is becoming.

Many kids go through a good deal of soul searching during this long vacation. They've finished the first half of the first year of college, and they may need to step back to take stock of where they are and what they want.

> *At Christmas I felt like the honeymoon was over for my son. He was thinking, Do I love the school, is it right for me? Even though he wasn't expressing all that, you could sense that these issues were there. It was great because my husband and I both had really good talks with him; he was doing a lot of "who am I?" stuff, a lot of questioning about lots of things.*

It's wonderful if your kid is ready to let you into his world this way. He may seem much more able to listen to your ideas and views, even if he doesn't agree with them. This is probably a big change from the discussions you had before he left for college, when he may have been so preoccupied with his own fears and concerns that he couldn't respond to anything you said. And the serious conversations you have now about the meaning of life may flood you with nostalgia for the philosophical discussions of your own post–high school years.

> *Hearing about my kid's first semester took me back to my own college experience; it's not exactly envy, but wishing you could do it over and avoid some of the things you did wrong.*

It's probably best not to overdo the "when I was your age" comments, but to let the discussion evolve at the level your child sets. Naturally your greater experience gives you a different perspective from his, but the big questions of life easily get submerged in the details of daily living, and it can be both stimulating and refreshing to think about them again and to hear your kid's ideas.

Don't worry, though, if your child doesn't talk to you about anything important during this vacation. He may need to retreat from the stress of college life and return to the comfort of familiar patterns. It may be a little too scary still, for him and perhaps for you, to move on to a new parent-child relationship. The change will come eventually, and meanwhile you can all enjoy a reprise of the not-very-distant past.

> *My daughter spent a lot of time at home during the vacation. It seemed like she was here, just hanging out, maybe with one or two friends, every night. She's a homebody; she really enjoyed just being home, having us around, seeing her old friends.*

The long winter vacation can begin to seem a little too long for some kids—and some parents, too. Part of the problem is that it's hard for kids to find jobs for only a month, especially because the before-Christmas hiring season is almost over by the time they get home. Many colleges make efforts to address this problem; some offer internship programs with alumni in the student's home area, for example, and other colleges have classes in January during the semester break, usually on campus. But if your kid isn't involved in such a program and hasn't found a short-term job, the time can hang heavy.

> *During semester break my son was bored out of his mind. There's nothing for him to do here, he just watches movies and eats, and it's totally unproductive. When he first got home he said, "This is great to have a long vacation," but two days before the end, his bags were packed, he was ready to go back.*

Though you probably agree that a bit of relaxation is well deserved after a semester of college work, you may grow impatient and irritable after a whole month of watching your child vegetate. To prevent this, you might consider investigating job possibilities before your kid comes home. Ask your friends, colleagues, and neighbors if they need a part-time (or full-time) worker during or after the holidays: baby-sitting, office work such as filing or answering phones, or one-shot projects like reshelving books in a library are jobs that college kids can do in January. And even if your kid protests, having a little structure to the days, as well as a little income, is likely to make the vacation more pleasant and certainly less boring.

For parents whose child has been unhappy at college, this vacation is a chance to learn more about what the problems are and how they might be solved. A mother offered advice:

> *If they decide they want to take a year off or transfer to another college, maybe closer to home, you have to be open to it. Sometimes it's in their best interest. Sit down and talk about the options, and then accept the choices they make, even if you don't agree with them. Sometimes you have to do that. But also you have to ask, "Why do you want to do this? Is it because you're lonely? Would it help if I come up to see you or if you come home for a weekend?"*

Sometimes a kid who hasn't settled in comfortably and found a niche decides to make the best of things, at least for another semester. Others are certain that they want to transfer.

When my daughter came home for vacation, she told us she wasn't happy at college and she wanted to transfer. I was concerned; every kid has an adjustment to make no matter what, and I wanted to make sure this wasn't impulsive, because it's often hard to be a transfer student. But she was so unhappy, we decided she couldn't go back.

It's not always easy to arrange a transfer to another college. Parents who have been through the process describe endless phone calls, lots of paperwork, and contacting what seems like a million people in a million different locations. And if credits from the first college are not accepted by the second, transferring can mean a substantial financial loss. For this reason, many parents try to convince a kid to return for the spring semester and then organize a transfer for sophomore year.

Often this isn't as cruel as it sounds. The second semester is only about four months long at most schools, and knowing that they can leave when it's over makes the prospect of sticking it out much more acceptable to many kids. In addition, waiting until the second year will give you and your child time to work out all the details and consider the available choices in a more leisurely way. More important, completing the second semester seems to give many students a new view of the college. By that time they "own" the campus, they've made friends, they may have met interesting professors whose courses they want to take. It's not unusual for a kid to decide to stay after all.

My son didn't get into his first-choice college, and he went to a school he considered definitely second best. From the first day, he planned to work really hard and then transfer after freshman year. But by the summer he loved where he was and he couldn't imagine leaving.

As the end of the vacation approaches, parents often find that their emotions are quite different from what they felt in September. They're not so worried this time around, and it's a good deal easier to see their kid leave for school. One mother said, "At the beginning you think, He's four hours away, oh my God; but by January you think, Four hours, it's nothing." Another parent said:

By the time the vacation ended in January I realized that this is the real thing, it's happened—whereas in August it was all so mental, I didn't know how it would be and I was confused and upset. Of course, I knew now how much I would miss her, but the mystery was gone—I knew what to expect. So my perspective on her leaving was one of more acceptance and reality than in August.

Parents also shamefacedly admit to a bit of relief as their child prepares to depart. During the first semester they've adapted to the child's absence, and having her home for a month or more has required some adjustment.

One day we were cooking and I started telling her where to find the vegetable steamer. Then I said, "Wait a minute—you live here." When she left, she was looking forward to getting back to school; she feels that's her life at this point. I had mixed emotions. It feels good when she's home, but it also meant disrupted sleep. You don't worry about them when they're away at college, and it's nice to get a full night's sleep again.

Many kids, especially those for whom college is the first sustained time away from their parents, experience the first semester of college as a dividing line. When they're home, they want to show their parents that they can take care of themselves now. They may expect their parents to behave differently toward them and treat them more as adults. Of course, the change is still patchy, and they're likely to swing between competent self-sufficiency and a more childish dependence and uncertainty. It's not always easy for a parent to keep up with the vacillations, but it's exciting to see your child taking giant steps into adulthood.

Summer Vacation

When summer rolls around, you're probably looking forward to having your kid home for three months or more. If you plan to pick up your child from college and drive him or her home, you may be taken aback by what you find.

> *Our daughter was one of the last to finish her exams, so hardly anyone was left in the dorm when we picked her up. I was really shocked—the place was a pigsty, with papers, dirty clothes, leftover food, and abandoned toiletry containers all over the halls, the bathrooms, the empty rooms. But what upset me most was the number of beer cans and even liquor bottles— they were everywhere.*

A sight like this brings it home to you that you don't really know much about the life your kid has been living at college, and the realization isn't always welcome. But as you help your child finish packing up, you may also realize forcefully that this is where his life is now.

> *It's amazing how much stuff they accumulate in eight months or so. It seemed like what we had taken up in September was half a van full, but what we brought back filled it to overflowing.*

At most colleges, the days when summer storage space was available for students are long gone. Maybe you're lucky enough to have a relative or friend near the college who is willing to stash the bulky items for you over the summer, or perhaps you'll decide to rent a self-storage space. But if not, you may wonder as you drive off where you're going to put all this stuff until next September, when you'll have to take it all back again.

Once you and your kid are home, there's likely to be a period of awkwardness as you all adjust again. A parent who teaches in public school said:

> *At the beginning of my son's summer vacation, I was still working and my younger kids were still in school, so he had nothing to do. His job hadn't started yet, and he was still on his college schedule, ready to begin the evening at eleven o'clock. My biggest problem was staying awake to talk to him, because I had to get up at six. The younger kids stayed up late to talk to him when they should have been studying for exams—I can't really blame that on him; they probably wouldn't have studied much anyway, but it was disruptive and hard to mesh our different lives. His life was on hold, he was in limbo.*

On the other hand, there may be some unforeseen advantages to having your kid home.

> *It was terrific for me. Before my daughter's job started, some nights she would make dinner for all of us. And before I went to work, I could leave a note for her about errands and other things that had to be done, like waiting for the plumber to show up. It was nice having someone responsible in the house during the day.*

But this period of being in between is often hard for kids; they've gotten used to being busy and keeping to a schedule. One student said about her first summer home from college:

It was nice to see some friends—and to have air-conditioning! But I missed the activities and the people at college. And once I got home, I was nervous that going back in the fall would be like going up there the first time—I knew it wouldn't, but I still had that fear.

For most kids, a summer job is both desirable and financially necessary. Many have already found work by the time they get home, but some spend the first couple of weeks in a job search. What's available varies widely, depending on where you live and other factors, such as transportation to a job site. Still, even if your financial situation doesn't require a summer job for your kid, you may think it's a good idea for him or her to contribute toward college expenses. Many parents feel that when their kid's earnings are earmarked for next year's "spending money," their child feels more responsibility for and investment in the whole process.

Summer school may also be part of your kid's summer plans, either to make up a course she didn't pass or to get a required course out of the way. You may be surprised at how expensive summer courses can be, and how quickly some of them fill up—it's a good idea to find out what's available and sign up early. Most important, though, is to make sure that her college will give credit for the summer course she plans to take. The rules about transferring credits are often complicated and rigid, so checking things out beforehand is a necessity.

Your friends and relatives will probably be eager to see your kid, and to find out how the first year of college went. Many students recall how tired they got of answering the same questions a hundred times. One took a novel approach to the problem.

I was so sick of saying the same things over and over, and then I had a brainstorm—I made a sign to wear like a sandwich board. Here's what it said: "I lost my tongue in a fishing accident—can't talk! Here's some help: State University. Sophomore next year. Haven't decided yet. Yeah, I like it a lot. Very nice kids. Yeah, a few pounds (not that you're so thin yourself). Good talking to you, too. Next, please." Actually, I didn't wear the sign—my mom would have been too upset. But I wanted to.

It's funny, and it's also truer than you might think. Noticing how many people ask the same unanswerable and overly personal questions will let you know what not to say when you talk to your kid's friends. And sharing a laugh about it with your child makes you aware that you're now often treating him as an adult rather than as someone much younger and less experienced than yourself.

What most parents notice during the summer is how different their kid seems. The contrast with the high school graduate they sent off to school in September is often striking. Your kid has probably chosen his courses for the fall semester and made plans for where and with whom he'll live when he goes back to college; you may suddenly realize that you didn't even know he was making these decisions, and you certainly didn't have any input.

When my son got home for the summer, he said casually, "I'm going to be living with three other guys in an apartment next year, so don't pay the fees for a dorm." I must have looked amazed, because he went on to explain that the four of them didn't get a suite in the dorm they wanted and then they heard about this great apartment and grabbed it before anyone else could. I was a little concerned about how he would manage, and I told him I couldn't imagine preferring to do your own cooking and cleaning. But then I decided, This is his life now, and he should live where he'll feel comfortable.

Another mother summed up her feelings when she said, "By the end of the first year I felt relief, a burden off my shoulders; what will be will be."

The change you're likely to notice most is your kid's increased maturity.

I'm beginning to look at my daughter as an adult from my gut, not just my head. I don't feel as responsible for her as I did; I'm looking at her choices in life as her responsibility. Of course, I'm always there to discuss things, but she's made a major shift, she's gone out into the world.

It's a different relationship from a year ago. This is not to say that she won't revert to a more childish mode from time to time or that she won't do anything irresponsible or stupid this summer. She probably will, and she may turn to you for help when there are problems at her job or when the car dies when she's driving it. But overall you may feel she's much closer to being a grown-up.

The summer after his first year, my son had a job related to my field, and it led to a lot of adult conversation and also to an understanding of what I do, which he hadn't had before.

Divorced parents often see changes in their continuing relationship with one another, as well as with their kid.

There was less and less need for communication between us about our daughter, because she was more and more able to take care of herself—at least I saw it that way. When she was in high school, every single thing was discussed between us, but by that first summer, there was very little we needed to talk about.

Another parent, whose marriage had broken up during the year, said:

My son has grown a lot—he's a different person, much more adult, with a better handle on himself. He knew there was a lot of tension at home, and he finally decided he needed profes-

sional help in dealing with it. Now it's clear he feels he can get on with his life.

When your child makes a major decision like this on his own, it's clear that he's taking charge of his life in a way that wouldn't have been possible a year ago. It can be a difficult realization for parents, who sometimes try to hold on to the control and the responsibilities longer than they should. Having a child who's an adult means you're older than you might wish or secretly pretend to yourself; you've moved into a different generation, and you may not like the idea.

But it usually doesn't work to try to stop the clock, and there's much to enjoy about having an adult child. Letting go of some of the responsibilities (gradually, of course!) can free you as well as your kid. Naturally you'll still have certain expectations, but you might try approaching them from a different angle. This summer, instead of telling your kid, "The rule is you have to call home if you're going to be out later than midnight," you might say, "I can't help worrying if you're out late and I haven't heard from you, and you might feel the same if I stayed out much later than you expected. So it will make life easier if we all agree to call and keep everyone informed." Putting things on a more even plane and explaining the reasons for your request make it clear that you know the relationship is changing, although the end result—your desire for a phone call—is the same.

Though it's rarely a smooth and steady climb, your kid's progression toward adulthood will continue through the college years. Sometimes you'll notice the change only when you look back and remember how things were a year or a few months earlier. Sometimes you'll regret the loss of your child's trusting dependence on you, but at other times you'll take delight in seeing what kind of adult is emerging.

CHAPTER TEN

Advice from a College Senior

by David Barkin

Looking back after three and a half years, I have tried to remember as accurately as possible what it was like to leave home for my first year of college and what I thought helped and hindered the process. Hopefully my recollections will help ease the often tense transition to college for other families. I have tried to keep in mind the overall college experience and how the details of my journey affected me through the rest of my college years.

The thing I remember most about the summer after senior year was the desire to hang out with my friends as much as possible. It seemed as if there would not be enough time to hang out and preserve the freedom of senior summer. Spending time with my close friends and with my girlfriend was more important than anything. It may have been selfish, but I don't remember worrying too much about how my parents would handle my leaving. I was too engulfed in my world of peers to think about much else.

Of course, this is only my own experience, and some kids may have a different point of view. But I would suggest allowing your kid to find closure with high school friends in his own way, without your getting upset at all the late nights. Although the end of the summer may not mean the end of the friendships, they do change, and it is necessary for the kid to somehow acknowledge this.

Near the end of the summer my friends and I began to reminisce about our years together in school. The future of our friendships was a frequent topic of late-night discussion. We worried together about whether the close bonds we had developed during high school would weaken without day-to-day contact. Couples who would soon be geographically separated also discussed what might happen to their relationships.

Over the whole summer my three closest friends and I, with our families, had gotten together four or five times at one of our houses for an informal barbecue or buffet-style dinner. As the summer drew to a close we had one final dinner. It was a nice way to get everyone together and have a final good-bye, and for me it was a reassuring reminder of the support I would have from home while at school. But for some people this might not be the best way to make the transition—some of my other friends preferred to have a quiet dinner with just their parents and siblings, rather than a "party."

Because my group of close friends was split up around the country, we saw each other only during vacations. This resulted in two realizations for me. One, I began to see that some of my high school relationships were mainly based on everyday contact and would not last without this frequent interaction. The other realization was that there were some relationships that I wanted to continue and that were strong enough to survive the distance.

I was disappointed that some of my friends in high school would probably not continue to be so close; I was happy that my closest friends did not fall into this category. However, in some ways the discovery that some of my high school relationships weren't based on much frightened me—I felt as though I might never make true friends. This fear was eventually put to rest both by the high school friends I did remain close with and by the new friends I made at college, but it was a genuine fear for a while.

The whole issue of packing turned out to be surprisingly stressful. For me there was a clash between my desire for independence (buying my own things and packing my own stuff) and wanting my mother to do it all so I wouldn't have to worry about it. I procrastinate often; however, that summer I took procrastinating to a new level. I never had time for packing—I always had something better to do. This was probably partly because packing is a pain, and also partly because psychologically I didn't want to leave the house sooner than I needed to. Packing was a big indicator that I was moving out for a long time. Looking back, I have tried to think about what might have eased the process a bit.

Although working with your kid and making a list of things needed for school may help, setting up a time for this can be hard. You may get those typical teenage responses—"Ma, I don't have time for this" or "Later, we'll do it later." But if you can spontaneously find a time, maybe one night quickly after dinner, it will be a step in the right direction. Trying to do this early in the summer will probably be next to impossible with most kids, although it would make things easier. But if you and your kid can't find any time at all together, you can always make the list of what you think he needs and then ask him to go over it and add anything. That should work with the more reluctant kids.

Once you have the list of things to buy, you may choose to put your foot down and tell your child when you both are going shopping or ask him when he would like to do it. Asking rather than telling is dangerous, because more than likely it will end up being his last day at home before he decides it's time to shop. However, dragging your kid around to stores is obviously no fun for either of you. Sometimes there isn't a good answer except to look for a compromise. And, of course, you may have a kid who loves to shop for anything and none of this will be a problem.

The last week before the "big day" is without a doubt hectic. Trying to get the last few nights of hanging out to mean more than they actually do is inevitable. Late nights are probable even if they haven't been a constant throughout the summer.

Packing is also more difficult than kids ever think. I was the type of kid who thought that the night before was too early to start packing. I figured we would just throw some stuff together a couple hours before we left. But with some nagging from my parents, I ended up having almost everything ready the night before. This was a definite plus. Having everything packed and squared away gave me time in the morning to really say good-bye to some important elements of my life: my dog, my few friends who were still home, and my house. Not having to worry then about whether or not I should bring my flashlight or pocket knife gave me time to feel as if I wasn't leaving anyone or anything out in saying good-bye.

When the big day finally arrived I wasn't very nervous because we weren't actually going to school that day—we planned to stay overnight with friends and then get to the campus early the next day. That night was when I got scared. All the unknown factors (Would I like my roommate? Would I make friends? Would the work be too hard?) came into my head as I was trying to go to sleep.

Some of my friends who made the trip to school in one day, rather than staying somewhere for a night, had different experiences. Don't be too worried if your kid exhibits some peculiar behavior on the last day. One of my friends, when I came over to say good-bye, was packing and getting stressed out. He walked over to the fridge, grabbed a beer, and chugged it down in front of his mother, at eleven A.M.! Another friend argued with his father about where each box and suitcase should be placed in the trunk.

Making the final day as stress-free as possible should be the goal, because every kid, as tough or as relaxed as they may appear, will be a little scared.

This is not to suggest that going to college is a hugely traumatic experience. But it is stressful, no matter how excited your kid is to get out of the house and into a new environment. Try to go with the flow of things and make the transition as smooth as possible. When your kid wants to pack the trunk of the car and you see him doing it in a way that doesn't make the most sense to you, try to let it go. If it turns out that the trunk space is really used poorly, suggest how it might be done a bit more efficiently. Don't get pissed off and say what an idiotic packing job your kid has done. Usually the trunk will be packed imperfectly but suitably, and by not making a big deal about it, you keep the stress level from increasing.

This applies to almost every trivial argument that could arise. Things that normally you might want to correct and take issue with, don't. Allowing your kid to do it his own way will make the trip smoother; it will also let your kid feel he's in charge of part of the process instead of being bossed around by the adults.

Once you get to school and unpack the car, look for cues that a kid will give you to disappear for a while. If the roommate is there and they are talking, butt out. I got very lucky and my freshman roommate became one of my best friends at school. However, the first day it was nice to have my parents go get "other things" (bookcase, hangers, etc.) while my roommate and I set up the room, talked, and got to know each other.

Depending on the kid, you may want to leave shortly after everything is out of the car. As hard as this is for a parent to do, if the kid says he wants you to get out of there, he usually means it. Hanging around will make the kid feel awkward, which won't do much for your comfort.

There are kids who want their parents around for a while, even for a few days. This does not mean on campus 24/7 [twenty-four hours a day, seven days a week]. But if you have a place to stay nearby, your kid may want to go out to lunch or dinner or just go shopping a day or two after he has moved into the dorm. Feel it out, but try not to wear out your welcome.

Although I do not remember feeling overly homesick, I did come home (from four hours away) on two or three weekends before Thanksgiving. I called home often, and although my parents probably think I told them nothing about what was going on at school, it was nice for me just to chat for a little bit. I think it's normal to call often and even come home a few times in the first semester of the freshman year. Don't read too much into these visits or frequent phone calls. They don't mean that your kid is having a bad time at school or not handling his independence well, they are all part of the adjustment process.

The same is true for a lack of phone calls and visits home. Kids deal with new environments differently; not calling home does not mean your kid has forgotten you, and it also doesn't mean he will never call you again. It probably just means your kid has become engrossed in college life and is looking forward to coming home and seeing you but is busy for the time being at school. This is a good thing.

One element of college life that I know many parents worry about is the accessibility of alcohol and drugs. This concern has been around for years and still prevails as one of the major issues discussed in politics on campus and off. I am not about to go into my personal opinions on these issues. That would be another book. What I will comment on is what I think is reasonable for parents to worry about.

At almost all colleges in the United States, even if they have dry campuses, alcohol and drugs are available to kids if they want to seek them out. Parents should not be fooled or naïve when they read the college course book where only a paragraph is devoted to the "legal" social life at the school.

Although Greek life may be on the verge of changing and varies from school to school, I found that where there are fraternities, there is pressure to drink. It is possible to be a part of the Greek system and go through pledging without drinking; it has been done, but it is tough. Even without Greek life, the fact is that college-age kids experiment with alcohol. As with other dangerous behaviors, peer pressure, especially for inexperienced freshmen, is pervasive.

Conversations with friends suggest that the prevalence of drugs and the types of drugs found on campuses vary from school to school and from region to region. My impression is that drinking is the most popular illegal activity for college students, but smoking pot is a close second on some campuses; use of hard drugs (hallucinogens, coke, and heroin, for example), as well as abuse of "study enhancers" like Ritalin and speed, are definitely present at more schools than parents might hope.

My advice to parents would be: *definitely* discuss drugs and drinking with your kids before college, and earlier if you feel comfortable. Do not give them the DON'T DO DRUGS speech unless that is exactly what you believe. Don't be hypocritical when it comes to drinking, either. If you drink wine with dinner or have a drink now and again, explain to your kids why you don't want them to do it.

More advice from a jaded senior: if you have trusted your child until now, don't worry too much; if you know or suspect that your kid has already experimented a bit in high school, don't worry too much. In any case try to be as open as possible to the issue. Explain why you might be worried and/or what you do and don't expect of your kid. But also expect that your kid may disagree with what you are saying, and may come home at winter break and fill you in on some things you may not want to hear. If you think your kid can handle the "college lifestyle," but you don't really want to know about it, don't worry, he probably can.

This particular section is not intended to scare any parents, including my own. Most kids handle the pressures of drinking and drugs without too much trouble. However, it obviously is an issue because some kids do not handle the pressure well and get involved in things they may not really intend to. Discussing things with your kid will help, but to be honest, your kid probably has already developed the behaviors and attitudes toward drinking and drugs that she is comfortable with, and there is not much you can do to change that.

Another worry for parents is dating and the pressures, anxieties, and freedom that come along with it in the college scene. This is a genuine worry for kids as well. Whereas in high school even the most unruly kids had to check in with their parents at some point, at college they're on their own. I would be lying if I said there are never any one-night stands, date rapes, or hooking up after drinking too much and regretting it in the morning. Although none of these are regular occurrences, most college students know someone who has had such an experience. I remember two guys in my Spanish class talking about a weekend party where they had gotten drunk and one had gone home with a freshman he'd met there.

On the other hand, several of my friends ended up being involved with someone for a long time. Although some of them are no longer together, they were able to steer clear of the promiscuous lifestyle. The reality is that it's not that difficult to resist the pressure, even if you don't have a serious girlfriend or boyfriend. And, as with drinking and drugs, your kid has probably already thought about dating and sex and has come to his own conclusions.

One other aspect of college that sometimes becomes an issue is grades. In my mind, once a kid gets to college, he has already formed his study habits, good or bad. A friend of mine who had breezed through public high school without much effort had some trouble at college. Because he was used to getting good grades without a lot of work, his grades suffered freshman year. College was a lot more difficult.

A few times during the semester, my friend's father came up to help him study. His father was a college professor and presumably knew the subject matter of my friend's courses. However, it seemed that instead of wanting to learn the subjects he was taking, my friend ended up trying to get decent grades for his parents.

Throughout the semester his parents were constantly asking about his grades. Of course, this was only a natural parental concern: They wanted their son to do well. However, both the constant pressure and the help my friend received from his father before tests were, I think, detrimental to his growth as a student. My friend was focused on getting grades that his parents would be pleased with, but he was also annoyed with the way his parents were acting. This is not what college is supposed to be about. College is supposed to be, first, a place to learn about things you are interested in, and second, a place to develop a sense of independence and responsibility. It shouldn't be a place where a kid learns how to continue to depend on his parents and only aims to please them.

Finally, I think both kids and parents wonder if their relationship will be affected when the kid goes to college. As I look back now, it seems that not all that much changed. But I remember thinking our relationship was a bit different when I came home for Thanksgiving and then for winter break freshman year. My parents seemed to think of me as more responsible and independent, and I felt as if I could speak to my parents and my parents' friends as an adult. I began to think of myself as closer to their level. They were no longer these distant authority figures who were leagues above me in terms of intelligence. One semester in college hadn't suddenly transformed me, but it did give me more confidence in my intellectual abilities.

As I have been writing this, it's been tough not to feel as though I am preaching. I'm now close to graduating, and it is hard for me to remember exactly what would have made my transition easier. To me, the fact that I can't remember all that much about the whole move to college suggests that it really wasn't that tough. My major piece of advice is that everything will eventually work out. The problems that arise seem very significant, and the moments can become very tense. But in the long run, at graduation you, and especially your kid, probably won't remember them— and if you do, they will seem trivial.

This is not to say that everything that comes up during this time is unimportant. But if you try to weed out the most significant issues and deal with them calmly, the transition will be smoother.

CHAPTER ELEVEN

A Few Last Words

As they look back on their kids' leaving for college, parents almost universally advise, "Try to relax and trust your kid to do all right." This is, of course, easier said than done—few parents can be truly relaxed as they bid farewell to their child—but the idea was echoed by many:

> *Let your child do what he wants within certain limits. If kids really feel the decisions are in their hands, it's better.*
>
> *Take your cues from your kid; each family, and each child, goes through the process a little differently. It takes time to find the right balance.*
>
> *It's very much the kid's journey. Work at giving your child leeway.*

This is exactly the advice offered by students as well, as you can see from the themes that run through the previous chapter. As they take the giant step into college, kids crave recognition and validation that they're not babies anymore; treating them in a more adult fashion helps them believe they'll do all right on their own.

Yet resolving the paradox of how to let go of their children and still maintain the family ties is a struggle for most parents. For some, the process of separating from their kids leads to new growth and discovery in their own lives, but for others it's enormously painful. Still, parents know that it's necessary; if they cling to their roles as controlling authorities and don't begin shifting toward a more equal balance, their child is forced either to remain a dependent child within that relationship or to break away dramatically in order to assert his independence.

The progression is not often smooth, and for each step forward there may be a half step back. Conflicting needs and desires tug at both kids and parents as they attempt to redefine their relationship. For students who live at home, the process is sometimes harder than for those who are away, because in a shared space it's so difficult to know how and when to change the rules and how to adapt to changing roles.

It's a daunting task for parents: letting a kid find his own way while also offering support.

> *Be there to be supportive. Your child may not ask for help or advice, so you have to be alert—but try not to step on his toes.*

> *You always have to be willing to listen, even if you don't like what you're hearing. No matter what time of night or day, show her that you can stop what you're doing and listen to her, and offer suggestions if they are wanted. I think if parents say, "Our responsibility is over now that you're in college," the kid misses that family support.*

> *You have to try to see their point of view; it makes kids less defensive and more ready to try harder. The most important thing is to keep the lines of communication always open.*

> *This sounds great, and if it were easy to do, everyone would be a perfect parent and would breeze through this tumultuous period without a care. But it's definitely not easy, and you may often find yourself laying down the*

*law or blowing up in anger when what you meant to do
was listen calmly and offer suggestions in a sympathetic
manner. The key word here is "try."*

Keep in mind, too, that even when your kid is driving
you crazy, he or she notices and appreciates your love and
concern. The previous chapter makes it clear that kids need
contact and support from parents, even if they have trouble
saying so.

Many parents emphasize the need to keep your expectations realistic. You may find that you've selectively edited
your memories of your own college experience, remember-
ing only the good parts and canceling any recollection of
the less-than-wonderful aspects; this may lead you to overwhelm your kid with upbeat enthusiasm and to downplay
or ignore his fears. On the other hand, you may be focused
entirely on your worries about your kid and your own anticipated loneliness. But it's more helpful to your child if you
can acknowledge that the first few weeks, at least, will be a
mixture of positive and negative for you as well as your kid.

*Painful as it is to give up your child, be aware of the
positive side—this is new and exciting for your kid. There
are things you can enjoy vicariously.*

*Especially if your kid hasn't been away from home much,
expect that you'll be lonely, and your kid will be, too.
Expect a period of uncertainty.*

*Your feelings may be really powerful at the beginning,
swinging from high highs to low lows in a single day.
But by winter vacation your emotions won't be so strong
or so close to the surface.*

*It helped a lot to talk to people who've been through the
process—my kid found it helpful, too.*

Finally, if you've been dreading the onset of the empty
nest syndrome, the reported experience of other empty-nest-

ers may make you feel better. In several studies, parents did not describe their child's leaving home as a crisis or as one of their lives' lowest points. Researchers had expected that parents, especially mothers, would see this as one of the worst times in their lives. They were surprised to find instead that "the satisfactions of parenthood continued for both sexes. The prospect of an empty nest seemed not to threaten the parents. . . . Rather, they looked forward to a somewhat less complex lifestyle with relief."

Each family, and each family member, experiences this period of change, turmoil, and readjustment in a unique way. And for nearly everyone there are times of unhappiness, questioning, and deep concern. But for most parents, any lingering fears and disappointments are soon outweighed by the positive feelings of excitement and pride as they watch their kids begin to establish themselves as independent, responsible human beings.

INDEX

Carol Barkin, a graduate of Harvard University, has written more than forty books for both adults and children. A native Midwesterner, she has lived outside New York City for twenty years. She and her husband survived sending their son to college, and gained a great deal of valuable and surprising information in the process.